THEME-SETS FOR SECONDARY STUDENTS

How to Scaffold Core Literature

JEANNINE D. RICHISON
ANITA HERŃANDEZ
MARCIA CARTER

HEINEMANN • Portsmouth, NH

#6242114q   3-23-06

Heinemann
A division of Reed Elsevier Inc.
361 Hanover Street
Portsmouth, NH 03801–3912
www.heinemann.com

Offices and agents throughout the world

Library of Congress Cataloging-in-Publication Data
Richison, Jeannine D.
    Theme-sets for secondary students : how to scaffold core literature / Jeannine D. Richison, Anita Hernandez, Marcia Carter ; foreword by Cris Tovani.
        p. cm.
    Includes bibliographical references and index.
    ISBN 0-325-00914-7 (alk. paper)
    1. Reading (Secondary)—United States.   2. Literature—Study and teaching (Secondary)—United States.   I. Hernandez, Anita.   II. Carter, Marcia.   III. Title.

LB1632.R52 2006
428.4071′2   2005034444

Editor: Jim Strickland
Production service: Melissa Inglis
Production coordination: Vicki Kasabian
Cover design: Jenny Jensen Greenleaf
Typesetter: House of Equations, Inc.
Manufacturing: Steve Bernier

Printed in the United States of America on acid-free paper
10   09   08   07   06   RRD   1   2   3   4   5

CONTENTS

FOREWORD

Waiting in a long line at the airport, I struck up a conversation with a man in his mid-forties. We shared our respective destinations and then quickly moved on to our professions. When he learned that I was a high school teacher, he sighed and said, "Boy, I'd love a low-stress job with three months off in the summer." I bit my tongue and told him that teaching could be quite stressful and teachers are rarely "off" for three months in the summer. I don't think he believed me.

When my flight took off, I was still stewing about his comments. I realized that it wasn't the teaching part that was stressful; it was all the things that interfere with trying to be a good teacher that bogged me down. Had I more time and patience, I would have shared with my airport friend a sketch of a typical middle school or high school classroom—one filled with thirty or more students who prefer instant messaging to literary analysis. I would have explained that many of the students sitting in that classroom are reading below grade level and would rather be almost anywhere than in an English class. I would have shared that often there are not enough materials to go around and that frequently teachers are stuck with thirty copies of the same novel that no one wants to read. I would have explained that each class period is only forty-nine minutes, not nearly enough time to address all the state-mandated standards. Explaining the part about school officials caring more about raising tests scores than teaching students how to think would probably be a waste of my breath. However, I might try to let him know that delivering information is pointless unless students know how to think and apply what their teacher has shared. No wonder we are so stressed out.

Yet everywhere I go, I meet dedicated teachers undaunted by the everyday interferences. They remain hopeful and eager to learn how to do their job better. One such teacher was Jeannine Richison, whom I first met while doing some work in central California. She was working with her university students to learn how to help students read and understand text better. Jeannine had heard of my work with struggling readers and wanted to know more about what I was doing. Now, reading her book, *Theme-Sets for Secondary Students: How to Scaffold Core Literature,* we have come full circle. It is I who am learning from her and her coauthors, Anita Hernandez and Marcia Carter. I am excited to be able to bring their fresh ideas back to my school, as well as to the learning communities throughout the country who continue to wrestle with literacy instruction at the secondary level.

Like most teachers, I didn't go into the profession to raise test scores. I wanted to share my love for reading—how I am moved by the written word and how it mirrors the human condition. Reading literature assures me that I am not alone in times of trouble, that someone before me has wrestled with a similar foe and survived. I want my students to know that they too can experience the power of being literate. Sadly, teaching students how to read and understand literature has taken a backseat to covering content standards and increasing proficiency levels. Sometimes the struggle to meet the diverse needs of resistant readers becomes incredibly stressful.

For teachers who are not yet ready to cry "Uncle," *Theme-Sets for Secondary Students* may be just the book they are looking for. It is smartly organized by themes that language arts teachers of all levels can relate to. Annotated bibliographies of accessible text pepper the book and offer alternatives to struggling readers and English language learners, while exposing them to the literary canon at the same time.

In *Theme-Sets for Secondary Students*, Jeannine, Anita, and Marcia reassure lovers of literature that they don't have to abandon the canon in order to differentiate instruction. Suggestions for theme baskets blend timeless classics with soon to be new favorites and engaging nonfiction. All of the selections work in concert to help students truly explore what makes us human. Purposeful activities encourage readers to delve deeply into the subject. With the ideas shared in each theme, learners of all levels can participate in reading, writing, discussing, and most importantly, thinking. Students can't help but feel gratified and invigorated by their success.

As a teacher reading this book, I excitedly turned the pages, thinking how I can immediately adapt the authors' ideas to improve my own instruction. *Theme-Sets for Secondary Students* nudges me to examine my own beliefs about learning. Sections of the book propel me to examine how I can provide opportunities for all students to read and enjoy literature and nonfiction. No longer do secondary teachers have to feel married to the classics and divorced from their students. *Theme-Sets for Secondary Students* bridges the gap. I invite you to turn the page and dive into a realm where literature meets the real world.

Cris Tovani

ACKNOWLEDGMENTS

Collaborating on a subject with so many diverse angles is a complex and time-consuming endeavor. In our work together, technology mediated the distance between us, but it also carried with it frustrations that could only be soothed by human interaction. What we couldn't accomplish in isolation, we accomplished together, but we do want to offer special thanks to our families and friends whose patience and forbearance deserve more than mere mention here. As well, our colleagues at Cal Poly, San Luis Obispo provided fertile grounds for our imaginations. The student teachers in the Single Subject Credential program in English at Cal Poly gave us an enthusiastic audience when we couldn't "hear" ourselves anymore. Then, as the reviewers' comments began to come in, we realized *their* eyes and fresh viewpoints gave us *more* to consider. We are grateful to them all.

Most of all, we want to acknowledge James Strickland, our diligent editor at Heinemann. A notable education writer in his own right, Jim helped us to see our own voices and to hear our own vision. We are fortunate to have had his strong presence as our heroic shepherd.

INTRODUCTION

These days, the public is treated to annual front-page coverage of their local school district's test scores, school by school, grade by grade, and savvy Realtors describe desirable home locations as "close to successful schools," which, not surprisingly, are defined as schools that have met the expected Adequate Yearly Progress goal. Teachers are in the spotlight more than ever, pressured to refine curriculum to accommodate embedded test preparation while teaching a diverse population of students to read with comprehension, write fluently, and think critically.

This diverse population has changed developmentally and demographically. Students with widely varying needs are staying in school longer and in greater numbers than they did even thirty years ago. Teachers are challenged to meet the needs of English language learners (ELLs),[1] high school students still reading at the fourth-grade level, students technologically savvy enough to fix the computers in our classrooms before the district tech person arrives, and others clawing their way to the top to gain admittance to the most sought-after universities . . . all in the same class in many cases.

Tragically, reading has lost its luster for too many high school students somewhere after elementary school, where high-interest books stimulated their curiosity and capitalized on their experiences or carried them away to new and enticing places to meet fascinating people they would like to know in real life. Society tends to blame the obvious culprits: interests that consume the time students formerly spent reading (television, sports, or the opposite sex), a loss of imagination stemming from reality intruding upon childhood, or, perhaps, a lack of adult role models who read as a significant leisure time activity. Even allowing there is some truth to this, these are scapegoats for more academic reasons. Despite the testing, a significant number of students continue to be left behind, and those who should be forging ahead deliver lackluster performances.

---

1. The term *English language learners* is used because it denotes a positive perspective of students who are learning English as a second language. The term *English as a second language* is used to refer to the instruction provided to English learners.

Although our student population has changed, adjustment in curricular choice and methodology has occurred slowly and sometimes painfully.

Grades have never been enough of an incentive to entice students through high school classics they see as being so remote from their own experiences that they simply refuse to attempt their homework reading. This causes the teacher to become frustrated when students come to class unprepared and to resort to reading the book aloud in class. On the positive side, oral reading of the book mitigates the literacy deficits of "marginalized readers" such as ELLs or those who have never progressed beyond decoding into meaning making. But the oral reading also enables another type of reluctant reader—the avid reader, one who comes from a print-rich home and seeks out books in their own interest areas to read on their own time. These avid readers often come to class with a book in hand; however, it is rarely the book the class is reading. They are bright enough to listen to class discussion, pick up a thread of meaning to which they can relate, make pertinent comments about issues but not necessarily the text itself, and put all the pieces together before being asked to write the practice essay on the assigned book. They wait for the teacher to tell them the "right" interpretation—what was important in the text and what to think about it, creating a "culture of literary dependence and subservience" that leads to the intellectual disenfranchisement of student readers (Blau 2003, 34). Too often these students lack engagement with the literature and are unwilling to do the work it takes to understand and interpret the text on their own, creating meaning that is of some value to them.

To reach both ends of the reluctant reader spectrum, we propose a classroom methodology that combines best practices using theme-sets to support the core literature. Theme-sets as we use them are collections of books from a variety of reading levels and genres that introduce the major theme (or themes) of a piece of literature commonly found in the high school canon. We begin with colorful, easy-to-understand books with sophisticated messages, moving through texts of increasing linguistic difficulty, improving students' confidence in full-text mastery, and moving them toward more sophisticated interactions with text. Students who, for any number of reasons, are not fluent readers and struggle with text will improve their vocabulary in a less stressful context by seeing words in books with pictures or books written at their current reading level, which require less of them in terms of comprehension but more valid reader responses and connections on the thematic level. Having familiarity with some vocabulary of the theme in the set will assist them in interpreting context clues in the more difficult text. Picture books and variable-level chapter books scaffold concepts of more difficult text by ensuring an accurate mindset from accurately detailed pictures and creating or supplementing students' background knowledge about the setting and theme (or themes) of the core text.

One of the most vivid metaphors for the confidence we would like to instill in our students is a literacy circle. Those who become comfortable with the printed word, both their own and that of others, are insiders—inside the circle. Many of our struggling readers and writers are on the circle itself, marginalized by their lack of fluency, able to see inside the circle but not quite able to step inside at this point. There are also those who through ignorance or disability do not even approach the circle's edge. Our hope, through the implementation of the best practices drawn together and described in this book, is to enable those on the circle's edge to jump right in and to lure those farther away on the outside itself to draw a bit closer.

Our goal is to provide opportunities to present texts with opposing authorial views, legitimizing resistance to text while still respecting it (Rabinowitz and Smith 1998) and helping students build a personal experience that is rich in texture and variety. We encourage individual reading, small-group work, and whole-class reading and participation, as well as student choice and effective, research-informed activities that capitalize on expression through multiple intelligences. We want students, no matter their ability level, to have the opportunity to show us what a text means to them. We will explain possible logistical ways to use our theme-sets, provide an annotated bibliography for five themes including potential works to include in your own sets, and suggest activities for the teaching of the core text that focus on using each of Gardner's multiple intelligences. The first theme-set on *The Grapes of Wrath* (Steinbeck [1939] 1967), a commonly used book in high school American literature classes, has been fleshed out more thoroughly than the others as a model for what could be done with the suggestions we offer. We do not wish to usurp individual planning for the core books or other books identified in a set but rather to enhance it by providing support prior to reading, thereby giving students a better chance at access to the literature.

We acknowledge that administrative approval for spending money on new books is sometimes difficult to get, especially when the lion's share of funds go to purchase anthologies that cost districts hundreds of thousands of dollars. Supplemental texts may even be an afterthought. We provide a research-based justification why such funds should be made available. If district- or site-level funds are still inaccessible, we will offer other suggestions to build theme-sets. Although none of the concepts embedded in our methodology is new, what we propose uses the best practices we know and have used for years to build new mind-sets in our students, both toward reading itself and their attitudes about the suggested themes.

Building such mind-sets is good for readers at all levels. More economically privileged students often have access to broader life experiences, such as travel and theater performances, enabling them to craft a mind-set beyond their own experiences. There is no guarantee, however, that these experiences will expose them to cultures or socioeconomic realities other than extensions of their own. Good readers, usually the linguistically advanced students, like to read and participate vicariously in experiences beyond their own backgrounds. Our theme choices extend the process of building mind-sets in contexts that students may not encounter in their own interest areas. They provide opportunities to develop understanding and empathy in students, extending beyond the mere visual framework for the era, geographical location, or lifestyle. The variety of texts offers students the opportunity to recognize objects and events in their own culture as well as in cultures distant from their own in time, place, and social class. But even more important than the chance to build new mind-sets about the world around them is the opportunity that becomes available to struggling readers to build a positive mental image of themselves as readers through their success at reading increasingly more difficult text and applying these successes to the core literature, becoming full participants in our language arts classrooms.

1 | USING BEST PRACTICES TO CONSTRUCT BETTER READERS

Tracing the cause of students' lack of engagement with classroom-assigned literature is difficult. Some feel it lies with the sincerity or commitment of the teacher or with the teacher's preparation in developmental reading strategies. Others feel it is caused by a disconnect between contemporary student experiences and interests and the texts they're asked to read. Still others say it is just a matter of the time available. As teachers are pressed to add the components of test preparation to their curriculum, districts and departments rarely decrease the number of literary pieces required to be taught at each grade level, and teachers find themselves supplementing the required reading with more duties, often taught in isolation from literature. Additionally, student reading aberrations (both at the skills level and motivation) force teachers to spend more time on each required core text because students cannot or may not do the required reading as homework. A writing component added to most district tests, and now even to the Scholastic Assessment Test (SAT), requires the assignment of more writing, which leaves even less time for new readings or new approaches. The vicious cycle continues.

"I'M A LITERATURE TEACHER, NOT A READING TEACHER"

Many high school English teachers (as well as content area teachers) believe children should have learned how to read in elementary school. These teachers, trained with strategies for dealing with the "product," are often bereft of strategies for teaching the process of reading. Early reading success is a foundation for later achievement, but reading development may be mapped on a continuum from early childhood into adulthood. Ideally, high school students continue to grow, learning to make sense of abstract, complex subjects far removed from their own experiences, whether this be in a chapter on cell structure in a science textbook or in a novel by Hemingway. Adolescents need to be guided to higher levels of literacy, not because their teachers in earlier grades failed to teach them appropriate reading strategies, but because literacy has many stages as a necessary part of reading development.

Young people who will function well as adults in the twenty-first century will need even more advanced forms of literacy than students in the past because they will read and write more than any population in history. They must be prepared to perform their jobs, operate functional households, make increasingly more difficult choices as citizens, and carry on their personal lives. "Adolescents deserve instruction that builds both the skill and desire to read increasingly complex materials" (Commission on Adolescent Literacy 1999, 5). Students probably already possess some basic reading strategies such as looking up a word in the dictionary or rereading passages that they do not understand, but learning how to handle increasingly difficult text is germane to our approach because progressing through increasingly difficult text is precisely what we advocate in our theme-set strategy.

Teaching practices that embody these strategies are integral to the theme-set approach we advocate. Although most people in this country can "read," that is, recognize letters and decode enough words in a sentence to gain a rudimentary understanding of what it says, many are not "readers." Learning to read and comprehend complex material demands certain strategies:

- questioning themselves about what they read
- synthesizing information from various sources
- identifying, understanding, and remembering key vocabulary
- recognizing how a text is organized and using that organization as a tool for learning
- judging their own understanding
- evaluating authors' ideas and perspectives (Commission on Adolescent Literacy 1999, 5)

"A reader is a person who makes particular kinds of intertextual connections, who asks particular kinds of questions of a text, who reads at a particular intellectual distance from the text, who talks about more than the text's meaning and analyzes its nature" (Williams 2004, 687). If we are not reading teachers, we are all teachers of readers, so where do we start?

ACTUALLY GETTING STUDENTS TO READ

Two components of motivating students to read seem so logical that they are unnecessary to state, but they are lacking in too many secondary classrooms. The first is time to read; the second is a variety of reading material that students can and want to read. More time spent reading results in corresponding increases in word knowledge, fluency, and comprehension. When students enjoy reading now, reading in the future is implicit and they may already be seeking out new materials to read, an encouraging harbinger of creating lifelong readers if only we can set the wheels in motion (Commission on Adolescent Literacy 1999, 5).

Providing a variety of reading material and spending time reading interconnected texts such as textbooks, websites, magazines, and paperbacks demonstrates in tangible ways how the world is also connected. Students learn to use multiple genres to fill in gaps in their knowledge and get a more complete picture of any particular phenomenon.)Reading across genres and media expands and strengthens their grasp of what is important to us as humans as well as helps develop thinking strategies to deal with both concrete and abstract problems.

Students, however, will not spend time reading if they are not provided with materials they can and want to read. Encouraging student choice in text selection and nurturing their developing competence in authoritative readings of their own moves them toward more sophisticated treatments of themes to which they can relate their own personal experiences. Students must work at learning to read. If students do not excel at the "process" of reading early on and experience the joy of books that unfold themselves to the reader, providing a panorama of places and people who enrich their lives, they will not experience the intrinsic rewards of reading, and they simply will not like to read.

Strong readers often take for granted their expertise and interest in reading and are willing to give the benefit of the doubt to text. Many books of the traditional literary canon require such a benefit of the doubt for average or language-challenged students. Advanced Placement or "honor" students have strategies that enable them to deal with sophisticated vocabulary and are able to ferret out thematic concepts that challenge their imaginations and sensibilities and so are as likely to have success with *The Scarlet Letter* (Hawthorne [1850] 1965) as *The Chocolate War* (Cormier [1974] 2004). Through critical analysis, they may even be able to find a connection between the "timeless" message and their own lives or the lives of those around them. Such is not the case with a significant number of secondary students.

The problem is that even strong readers, who are able to perform the tasks using a traditional, canonical work, admit they do not enjoy reading most classroom-assigned literary works. If students are able to "fake read" their way through high school, in Cris Tovani's words (2000), and choose to do so because they do not like the books we ask them to read in the classroom, there is something wrong with either our selections or our methods of teaching those selections (or maybe wrong with both).

Reluctant classroom readers may love to read books outside of the classroom; however, free-choice reading may not even meet with their satisfaction because teachers discourage students from reading books they feel are a waste of their students' time. Some children are strong readers but choose less challenging material when left to their own devices.

Readers will develop the interests, willingness, and abilities to take on more sophisticated literature if they have first had the opportunity to experience the pleasures of text that is meaningful, safe, and engaging for them. Young people often go through stages of reading when they are drawn to a particular type of book, author, or genre; readers of all ages find comfort in a familiar set of characters or a predictable plot sequence. Readers move on to more challenging material when their literary maturity demands it. In the meantime, familiarity with text helps readers develop speed and skill.

"Readers need to have books that understand them as they are and help them to consider and perhaps outgrow their current points of view. Then they will have the desire to deepen and expand their experience. Maturity entails, first, the recognition that you have a unique perspective and a view of the world that has value, and second, the recognition that there are different perspectives in the world and that these are worth knowing about, too" (Wilhelm 1997, 35). Any text that serves these ends ought to be recognized as literature—both literature written with students in mind and literature from the traditional literary canon. Multicultural literature, in particular, helps students enter other perspectives. To reinvent adolescent literacy, we need to draw from texts that adolescents value (Moje et al. 2000, 6). Two of the later stages of literary appreciation—"losing oneself in a story" and "finding oneself in a story"—happen only if adolescents can relate to a book in some way (Donelson and Nilsen 1996, 38–40). Students need books that include multicultural literature, which reflect their own experiences and those of their peers—that is, "literature by and about those members of groups considered to be outside the socio-political mainstream of the U.S." (Sims Bishop 1993, 39). If literature acts both as a mirror and a window into students' own experiences, their peers, and U.S. society, then multicultural literature reinforces and dignifies individual and group background experiences (Sims Bishop 1993, 41).

Students need multiple forms of representation; often readers with learning disabilities or second language issues become frustrated with traditional text and give up. Such negative experiences cause them to develop a resistance to reading traditional texts. These same students, however, read media texts with ease and embrace alternative representations such as drawings, film, cartoons, and photographs. They read books generally thought of as belonging to popular culture; in fact, the burgeoning young adult fiction market breaks sales records each year.

So, yes, secondary students can and do read. Furthermore, even if we teach a more traditional curriculum, there is no reason our students cannot be both successful and enthusiastic. We believe teachers can address the needs and interests of all students. Theme-sets, as we propose their use, utilize heterogeneous student-led literacy circles that read thematically linked books to visualize the theme, create and access background knowledge, and scaffold the traditional core text. Access to the great themes of the literature is made more readily available through inquiry and shared discussion. Additionally, we take into consideration the need of our diverse student population to see themselves in books and to participate in activities and assessments they choose that clearly illustrate the connections they've made between the text and the past and/or present world around them, demonstrating a critical level of reading comprehension.

Teachers know which texts constitute great literature, but many students do not need great art so much as great stories; they need the flame of interest lit by reading ordinary works that serve as jumping-off points for philosophical discussions (Milburn 2001, 93). When students are offered "good reads" from which to choose to propagate those discussions, the interest in the topic, as well as increased fluency stemming from time spent reading and the independence gained through successful reading, will serve to stimulate interest and intellectual investment in more classic core texts. Our goal is for the great literature to become the literature students can and will want to read.

SUPPORTING CORE TEXTS WITH CHILDREN'S AND YOUNG ADULT LITERATURE

Marginalized readers, especially those with learning disabilities or second language issues, often become frustrated with text and give up. As is the case for most people at any stage of development, teenagers usually shy away from activities that reinforce feelings of failure. Struggles with decoding that lead to embarrassment at not being able to read aloud smoothly add social pressure to an already diminished level of self-esteem. Although decoding problems are less frequent at the secondary level, many secondary students have poor reading comprehension or, at the very least, have not yet become "readers." Finding books all students can read and not insulting them in the process is key to their success. When asked about their literary life beyond the classroom, many less proficient readers have little or no recollection of being read to as children. Apart from being left out of the bits of mainstream cultural literacy that literary characters in picture books such as *The Cat in the Hat* (Dr. Seuss 1957) and *Madeleine* (Bemelmans 1958) bring to our lives, these students missed the extended practice of visualization of the story world by making the connection of text to picture. Without visualization when they read, students cannot experience and think about what they have read. Many express incredulity when asked what they are "seeing" or when they hear other students describing what they visualized while reading. They have low expectations of print and no sense of what readers do to make their print experiences meaningful. Coupling both decoding and comprehension issues, many English language learners struggle with language acquisition itself and never get beyond the meanings of words to see the world of the story. (We explore the literacy needs of our multicultural population in a later chapter.)

The ability of readers to visualize as they are reading is central to differentiating good from poor readers. In fact, the mental processes of readers of literature involve the continual triggering of a great symbolic system. Imagery plays a large role in helping readers formulate the thoughts that contribute to the meaning of the text. Viewing pictures connected to the text in books written for readers at any level assists in the formation of images, opening their minds to the possibility that words paint pictures and helping them formulate accurate images of what may be foreign objects from another culture or time period. Children's picture books are especially useful in this process because of their brevity, their beautiful and varied illustrations, and the compelling messages many convey. (Many of the books cited in our bibliographies defy age-appropriate designations because the format is deceptively simple, but they house mature and possibly, at times, disturbingly thought-provoking content.) Students given assignments that capitalize on the images portrayed in the text recall the picture in connection with the message, which then jump-starts the habit of creating their own images from text in books without pictures. The ageless appeal of beautiful illustrations and fond memories of these books voiced by more experienced readers in the class dignify the use of picture books for students who will benefit the most from reading and processing them.

Richly textured canonical literature is, by its nature, layered in meaning. Like poetry, each word carries a depth of interpretation that adds to the common message or messages each reader deduces from the reading. However, many of our high school students cannot access that literature, either because they cannot understand the language used or because they cannot decipher the significance behind the language used. Another important aspect of our scaffolding methodology is bridging students' prior experiences to the core text to be studied. Because our classrooms are microcosms of our country, teachers cannot assume that all children come in with the same background and basic knowledge. It is incumbent upon teachers to use their skills to provide the missing links, and when literacy is the goal, we have to scaffold the reading tasks we ask the students to perform. To create meaningful connections with the literature, students must be given opportunities to access their own similar background experiences and when the experiences in the literature are not linked to their own, to build that knowledge. In this way, teachers enable them to gain entrance into the story world of a difficult text.

Our state standards demand that students have an acquaintance with the great ideas of the world in general and American literature in particular, so our multiple reading strategies can assist in the reading of those ideas.

As less proficient readers using our theme-sets build fluency through practice with purposefully assigned books read by all students in the literacy circle, they will become more capable of reading and understanding the core selections that previously they may have "fake read" or not attempted at all. Using theme-sets in a classroom, teachers can utilize all the elements of universal themes to provide students of differing abilities access to great ideas of the literary world. Advanced students as well as lower-level readers will be given the means to access the literature together, collaboratively.

SHARED INQUIRY

Picture a typical high school hallway as it might appear between classes. Students might be rushing to get to their next classes, but no matter how much time there is before their next class begins, many of those students are gathered in small groups, everyone listening and talking. Their faces are animated and interested. They are turned toward whoever is speaking, and their body language indicates they are hearing what is spoken, encouraging further conversation. Whatever they are discussing, it probably isn't the Pythagorean theorem. When the bell rings, they part reluctantly. Their natural inclination to share with each other conversational topics that have meaning for them is similar to literature circles, a student-led discussion method for working with a commonly read book, that assists students in "connecting with books [read in common], taking responsibility as readers and group members, construct-ing meaning together, and beginning to debate and challenge one another" (Daniels 1994, 4). Students can gain far more from this type of discussion of their reading than they can from reading individually and reporting orally to the class, mimicking summaries that appear on the book jacket of their novels.

With the literature we offer our students in the classroom, we offer shared understandings of universal themes, whether our students are reading below, at, or above grade level, and no matter whether they have ever traveled down Route 66 during the Dust Bowl years, as in Steinbeck's *The Grapes of Wrath* ([1939] 1967), or are living in a small town in Alabama, as in Lee's *To Kill a Mockingbird* (1960). That we can expose our students to vicarious experiences through the literature is a long-accepted practice in our English-teaching profession.

DESIGN OF THEME-SETS

If we mix differentiated instruction (King-Shaver and Hunter 2003; Gregory and Chapman 2002) with literature circle pedagogy (Daniels 1994; Daniels and Steineke 2004), we can create "theme-set" pedagogy—reading assignments based upon themes, using a variety of texts on a variety of reading levels—that students can work with to gain access to significant ideas and themes. Using many texts on several different reading levels as the basis for grouping, students can be grouped to accommodate their level of understanding, which will allow them to take an active part in their own learning, participate in shared reading of the materials, discuss the enduring literary and life concepts they encounter, and become more likely to "achieve literary and intellectual independence" (Daniels 1994, 23).

In theme-based collaborative literacy circles, our students could discuss a series of texts with the same general themes, using a variety of children's lit-erature and young adult literature and with an anchor or core text from the body of literature we call "the canon." To provide examples of theme-based text sets, we develop five general themes with suggestions for children's and young adult literature with the same basic themes as the anchor novel.

INQUIRY-BASED TASKS

Complex themes and key issues emerge as students read and discuss their books within their groups. We now realize that students must come to their shared understandings through inquiry encompassing higher-level questioning, examination, and discussion. Students experience the texts through their shared experiences with each other and what they discover about the text and according to what they already know. This means the tasks assigned to students involved in using the theme-sets to discover theme must be differentiated and designed to build upon personal backgrounds.

For example, migrant students of today have an easier time identifying with the Joads in *The Grapes of Wrath* because they have experienced the necessity of following the crops as their parents travel to find any kind of work to provide for their families. Conversely, the majority of students, especially those from more affluent backgrounds, may not be able to identify with the desperation that the Joads face in their efforts to survive. The challenge then is to design common discussions that will focus on the essentials of the themes in the novel and in the collection of books in the theme-set. Projects designed to provide higher-level thinking will enhance the discussions. So an effective project that might be given to a group reading *The Grapes of Wrath* as its anchor text might be:

> Your group members are curators in a museum in which artifacts from the time of *The Grapes of Wrath* are to be displayed. Determine the ten best artifacts that would most represent the economic and personal hardships people faced during the Dustbowl era. Prepare a label for each artifact, and list the donor and the history of each artifact.

It is not hard to imagine the quality of discussion that results from this assignment, especially if the following is added to the assignment:

> The *Bakersfield Californian*, the local Kern County newspaper, carried the story of the local farm association trying to ban *The Grapes of Wrath* from classrooms throughout Kern. They felt that the story of the Joad family was unacceptable and books should be banned from Kern County libraries and classrooms that did not present a flattering picture of the Kern County farm owners. Considering this, create some artifacts that fairly present the controversy of this time and, yet, that are true to the story of the desperate migrating families.

Students who immerse themselves in a thought-provoking, relevant engagement with an assignment to be completed together experience both higher-level thinking and support from one another in their understandings.

ALIGNING WITH STANDARDS

Not all assignments are effective strategies. Students may show engagement with literature by creating dioramas and/or family shields, but what was the purpose, and how does it contribute to the value of the literary experience? These are critical questions, particularly because lessons of today must be standards-based, carefully planned right down to the assessment, and aligned with required testing.

Curriculum is much more carefully prepared than ever before as the students' future educations as well as federal financial support for their schools are at stake. Standards-based teaching is critical because, as we said at the outset, success of any curriculum is measured by the testing numbers. Students are expected to apply what they have been "doing" to a standardized test so that the school and district can disaggregate the resulting data into columns, rows, and positive results. As a nation, we expect measurable results and adherence to established standards. It is in this atmosphere, however, that our students need our expertise more than ever before. Any academic activities not aligned with standards are either not assigned or not allowed. Effective instructional activities should not only guide students toward competency and beyond but invite choice and use of students' skills and "strongest" intelligences, so they can demonstrate analysis of literature and literature's connections to life. Some types of instructional activities that been shown to improve student achievement include:

1. identifying similarities and differences
2. summarizing and note-taking
3. reinforcing effort and providing recognition
4. homework and practice
5. representing knowledge
6. learning groups
7. setting objectives and providing feedback
8. generating and testing hypotheses
9. cues, questions, and advance organizers (Marzano et al. 2001, 1)

These instructional strategies encourage students to demonstrate their understanding of the enduring relationships in literature and to develop critical skills linking school to life. Activities fitting the above nine categories are suggested in each chapter at the end of each theme-set. These strategies will guide students toward a positive interaction with literature and with each other. These general activities will guide the design of more specific learning situations, such as the specific activities modeled in the Migrant Families theme-set.

Students retain 10 percent of what they read, 20 percent of what they hear, and 30 percent of what they see, but they retain 70 percent of what they talk over with others (Stice 1987). If our lessons are designed to have students read and then discuss what they read with each other, does that mean that our lessons have been designed for maximum learning? Although this might appear effective in some cases, if this is all that happens in a classroom, it makes for bored, uninvolved students. The following chapters propose activities that focus upon effective learning informed by Howard Gardner's theory of multiple intelligences (1983) and Marzano and colleagues' *Classroom Instruction That Works* (2001). In each category, you may notice that the activities represented overlap into other categories. Just as there is a range of intelligences, our abilities to create responses to literature are not limited to one category because we are as intellectually diverse in our thinking as we are in our appearance. The nine instructional Marzano strategies previously listed are represented in the compilation of activities listed for each theme-set. The tasks are much more than simply expanded activities; they are designed to increase student understanding of the themes.

For example, setting objectives and providing feedback are techniques applicable to any grade level, any subject. Using the previously proposed assignment on *The Grapes of Wrath* as an example, the written response that results from the selection of museum artifacts could be scored using a criterion-referenced rubric. When students know the parameters of an assignment, cooperatively decide on the elements within the assignment, and discuss each element as it is selected, students' responses to such assignments can be given a rubric score. This type of feedback is especially effective because the students know before they start what level of achievement is expected and the standards for this achievement. The more specific the feedback, the better students are able to target their skills (Marzano et al. 2001).

Additionally, our assignment suggestions that accompany each theme-set are rooted in multiple-intelligences (MI) theory (Gardner 1983, 1993). Gardner identified seven (now eight) intelligences or capabilities that everyone possesses but in varying degrees, which include:

- linguistic intelligence (the ability to use words and connections to words)
- bodily-kinesthetic intelligence (the ability to create meaning through tactile means, such as creating handmade textiles, crafts, and the performance body motions such as dancing, athletic activities, and so on)
- spatial intelligence (the ability to perceive and repeat patterns and visual experiences)
- musical intelligence (the ability to create and relate musically through rhythm and sound)
- logical-mathematical intelligence (the ability to understand logical structures)
- intrapersonal intelligence (the ability to perceive and be attuned to one's own highly refined inner strengths and emotions)
- interpersonal intelligence (the ability to perceive others' moods and emotions and to use this ability to enlighten or persuade others)
- naturalist intelligence (the ability to "read" the natural world including that of living creatures and ecosystems)

Because Gardner's theory has application to the classroom, we identify and delineate those activities that address the capabilities of each intelligence. Several examples of MI activities accompany each theme-set. However, because the activities are examples, teachers are encouraged to alter or create new activities that address their own particular students, classroom habits, and personalities as the need arises.

In our text you will find five theme-based text sets. Each set includes an anchor text—from the canonical body of literature that is common to students in American classrooms—and the rest of the theme-set, which includes a selection of very easy and visually stimulating children's picture books as well as high-interest children's chapter books along with more demanding young adult literature. Students within any one collaborative literacy circle can access all the great themes of the set through exposure to books written on multiple ability levels. In role-based response groups, students read, respond, and immerse themselves in shared study of the material and create meaning using a research-based variety of responses, tested in real classrooms with real students. We also provide suggested activities designed to elicit thoughtful response and discussion on the themes common to the study of these higher-level texts. Some theme-sets have activities that are more specific to the actual core text, and others are more general and thematically linked. We want to provide teachers with models of the types of activities that may be assigned by drawing from the multiple intelligences while giving them the flexibility of choosing a different text from our theme-set or one of their own.

The use of theme-sets makes the actual literary ideas accessible to all students, even those whose comprehension is low enough to need remediation. If students are creating their own meaning, and in the process, they are discovering their own literary power, they cannot "behave like consumers of literary interpretations rather than the producers of them" (Blau 2003, 20). Once they see how they themselves relate to the texts, they are already into the important process regarded as "inquiry." The use of theme-sets becomes a pathway to success for all students into focused, academic tasks that build critical thinking skills and self-confidence.

2 | MAKING THEME-SETS WORK

Theme-sets, as we use them, are meant to work in heterogeneously grouped classrooms, as either an organizational methodology for using literature circles for supplemental reading or as scaffolding for required core literature that may be beyond the reading ability or interest of many of the students in our classes. In addition to the core literature selection, theme-sets contain texts progressing from children's picture books through children's and young adult chapter books, poetry, nonfiction, film and visual images, and beyond, if appropriate.

ORGANIZING THEME-SETS

To use a theme-sets approach with the teaching of core literature, students are grouped in fours, and each literacy circle receives the same books in their theme-set baskets. Four students per literacy circle seem to be the most easily manageable logistically. This arrangement also facilitates active roles for each student; it is easy for less vocal students to shy away from involvement in larger groups. If a student is absent, three participants still give each a feeling of group involvement, whereas two feels more like a think-pair-share type of activity, which teachers often use to facilitate involvement of English language learners.

Though any container large enough will work, a sturdy stackable plastic or rubber container with a lid works best to hold the books. Each "basket" typically contains:

- one copy of each picture book (teachers may include five or six different titles)
- one copy of each children's chapter book (again, teachers may choose to include five or six different titles)
- four copies of each young adult chapter book
- four copies of the core literature selection
- one copy of each advanced reading selection
- one copy of each nonfiction or nontraditional text

PROCEDURE

Every literacy circle member should read each picture book. The picture books are by far the most costly addition to the theme-sets. Because groups will be reading these books in class, the picture books may be checked out from a local public library or borrowed from local district elementary school libraries through the district librarian. Not allowing the books to go home with students prevents the "double checkout"—when a student loans a checked-out book to another student without notifying the teacher in advance—that often results in lost books. (If students from a period early in the day are allowed to take a book home, it would be wiser to have them pick it up after school; otherwise that book will not be available to other classes later in the day.)

Some literacy circles may choose to read picture books aloud; others might select a book apiece, read their selection, and pass it to the next person in the group, rotating through all the books. Most baskets will probably contain five or six picture books although we have included many more in our theme-sets so teachers have a selection from which to choose. This more extensive listing should make it easier to find books for those teachers who decide to borrow them. The reading of the picture books will probably be completed in one class period. At this point, most likely on day two of the unit, literacy circles discuss possible themes for the set of picture books. The theme should be present in all of the books. Students are often amazed at how many layers of meaning may be found in what appears to be a very simplistic book for young children. When they are able to discuss the underlying meaning of the collection of texts, they quickly lose the attitude that "these are baby books." The length of time spent on the post–picture book process can vary as long as teachers feel that meaning is still being created from the experience. If the possibility exists for a summative choice assessment, students could create their own picture books, either as an end in itself or as a gift to a child in a neighboring elementary school, and many students have expressed an interest in this option. More time may be spent analyzing book formatting, types of illustrations, or any literary element the students need.

The second step in using the theme-set approach involves students individually selecting one of the children's chapter books from their basket. This book will be issued to the student, who takes it home to read at his or her own pace over the course of a week. During the time that students are reading their books outside of class, teachers may either provide "intro" assignments for the core literature piece in the set or teach grammar, vocabulary, short writings, anything that district or state standards demand, much of which can be related in some way to the theme of the theme-set. These assignments may involve video, non-literary selections, technology, or even visual arts and music. On the day the chapter books are to be completed, students return them to the basket and work in their groups on some unit-related activity. Teachers may have individual students present to the literacy circle group something of the plot and themes in their chosen books. The list of themes the groups generated after the completion of the picture books may now be expanded, or possibly narrowed, to include those the students discovered in their chapter books.

The children's chapter book is followed by the selection and reading of one of the young adult chapter books. These are well-written, high-interest books that usually result in a relatively quick reading. Teachers may use the same young adult book for every member of the class or let students choose from among several. The methodology chosen will result in different types of classroom activities to supplement the reading. Depending upon the class and its collective reading level, teachers may even decide to have the young adult book be outside reading while the class begins the core text in class.

At this point reading to scaffold a core selection departs from reading as an outside activity supported by the use of literature circles. If you are using theme-sets to promote reading and discussion of self-selected titles, your set should include several thematically linked popular titles as well as works from the canon and from genres other than fiction. How you choose to use those is as varied as the titles you may select as your whole approach is to supplement classroom reading with student-choice books.

To continue the use of a set for scaffolding a canonical work in high school, all students are assigned the reading of the core text after the completion of the young adult novel. We have provided activities for each theme-set that offer opportunities for all students to participate and experience success. These activities have been designed expressly for the teaching of the core text, but they could be applied earlier in the process with few modifications. An assignment that could have perhaps the greatest impact is the negotiation within the group of a theme statement to span all of their texts. We require a "statement" because it demands much more critical thinking to word a sentence that is accurate and meaningful than to just tag it with a word or phrase, much as we have done in the titles of the theme-sets. Once each literacy circle has arrived at a single theme statement, the students may do research to find an historical example or current event that exemplifies their chosen theme, an activity that students of all ability levels will be able to participate in with the support of their literacy circle and some freedom of choice in mode of expression. When students find historical and contemporary pieces that depict their themes, they may add them to the theme-set. (We suggest that single-page additions be laminated for prolonged use.)

More skillful readers may choose to supplement their reading with one or more of the more challenging texts, others with nontraditional, multigenre selections. Nontraditional works may include nonfiction, newspaper and magazine articles, Internet selections, artwork, graphic novels, and the like. At the high school level, Advanced Placement texts as well as nonliterary texts, which often appeal more to young men than fiction, may be included.

ASSESSMENT

The summative assessment with theme-sets and core literature selections may take several forms. Teachers usually require some sort of unit examination as well as an essay. In addition to the traditional linguistic assessments, we recommend a choice assignment done either in a group or individually. We believe the oral component of such a project is important for the students' full development.

DO STUDENTS WRITE IN JOURNALS?

One question often asked by those interested in our theme-set approach is whether we have students write in journals during the unit. Journals have become such a common activity in classrooms that we find our students are bored with the process and groan at the mention of them. They can also be intrusive in the reading process. Our in-class writing generally occurs during the course of some book-related activity. On occasion we may ask students do a quickwrite at the beginning of class that could be written in their journals, but during the reading of the picture books as well as the children's and young adult chapter books, we do not require journal writing. Our goal is to encourage fluency and a love of reading.

As adults, we seldom write in a journal during or following a session of reading for enjoyment. If we knew that we had to write after each time we read, we might never pick up a book because of the time such reflection would demand. Though we might take some notes on our thoughts in a more spontaneous way, especially if we participate in a book club, when we are truly reading for enjoyment, we are much more likely to want to talk to someone about what we read. We want our reading process in the theme-sets to follow as closely as possible the behaviors of lifelong readers. Of course, teachers who choose to teach thematically using a theme-set may decide to add in any type of process writing they feel is necessary.

IS A SYLLABUS NECESSARY?

People interested in our process have also asked if we hand out a detailed syllabus of sorts to students at the beginning of each unit. When we introduce the concept of the theme-set, we give students only a very general overview. If we have numerous students who are reading below grade level and we tell them that they are going to be reading as many as eight books over the next few weeks, they may give up before they even begin. Only later, after students have enjoyed and experienced success with one theme-set unit, do we feel an overview sheet would be appropriate for the next unit. At the beginning, we do give them a project choice list for the summative assessment, so they may begin thinking about what they would like to do. Although they cannot begin the assignment until they have read a substantial portion of the core text, we find that giving students the choices up front is appealing because ours are so different from the traditional essay as the end-of-the-book assessment to which they are accustomed. The anticipation of a creative assignment that capitalizes on their strengths often generates even more interest in the unit.

FINDING THE MONEY

One of the most critical questions about developing theme-sets is: How do we find money to buy additional texts in the ever-dwindling budgets of most schools, especially when these sets fall under the category of supplementary texts? In our experience, English departments tend to continue to buy books that they already have copies of, generally the core selections that would be included in the sets anyway. You may be able to generate enthusiasm and a portion of your department's funds for a new approach to teaching literature by showing how this approach meets the needs of diverse groups of students and facilitates successful literature units with the most marginalized readers in your classes. We have included in our book some of the available theory to support such a claim, not because you need to be exposed to the theory to experience the benefits of the process but because we know that administrators and school boards want substantiation that their investment of taxpayer funds in a new idea will be profitable for students. If decision makers do not use research to justify their curriculum mandates, wouldn't it be a refreshing change to be able to offer such a justification in your well-thought-out request?

We understand that initially the capital layout for such a methodology as ours could be quite costly, but we believe the results are spectacular and will warrant that eventual expenditure. Your biggest investment of time is in locating the books. If you borrow them during your first experience with theme-set units, we believe you will find ways to buy sets of books that will be yours to keep. We have already suggested local and elementary school libraries in your district as good sources for children's picture and chapter books.

Librarians want their libraries to fulfill a need in their students' lives. It has been years since we have seen school librarians in a classroom doing book talks to get students excited about new titles. High-interest books generate their own hype both inside and outside of class. School librarians often ask for book titles when they are ordering for a new year. Some librarians have the misconception that students are only interested in nonfiction sources and the Internet for research purposes. Librarians want students to read fiction. Work together with them to see if you can get multiple copies of books that may be on loan to you for a few weeks. Requesting titles librarians know students will be reading has the potential to produce the young adult titles you need for your sets, even if they are only on loan to you.

Once you have permanently collected what you need, you will have the choice of updating the sets when new books using your theme are brought to your attention or come on the market. Our local Rotary Club has been very supportive of our schools and is willing to underwrite whole baskets of books. Other community service organizations, especially the American Association for University Women, as well as your Parent–Teachers Association (PTA) or Booster Clubs may also be willing to buy one or more baskets. Bookstores also offer discounts to teachers for books they will be using in the classroom. Because the theme-set approach is so viable for English language learners, your administrators may see it as a beneficial use of Title I funds. We have seen numerous monies frittered away at the end of the fiscal year because of the "use it or lose it" spirit of accounting. If you price the cost of a complete basket of books, you could request as many as the remaining funds in the budget will support. Keep records of increased test scores, something district and local administrators understand best, especially improved reading scores of your reluctant readers. Demonstrate success and it will breed support from many fronts. It is the first baskets that are the hardest to come by.

3

THEME-SET 1:
MIGRANT FAMILIES

Core Text: The Grapes of Wrath
by John Steinbeck

The plight of migrant farmworkers continues today; many migrant farmworkers live and work throughout the United States, picking the fruits and vegetables that Americans and others eat as well as grapes and hops many consume in wine and beer. The following theme-set is particularly appropriate for our students, and because the Steinbeck classic, *The Grapes of Wrath* ([1939] 1967), is core reading for many eleventh graders, our theme basket meets multiple needs. We are aware that not all teachers have experience with students from migrant families; however, residents of California's central coast, rich in fields of produce, are familiar with the coming and going of their students throughout the academic year as their families pursue the seasonal work of picking cabbage, lettuce, and strawberries, much as the Joads are forced to do in *The Grapes of Wrath*. The 1930s Dust Bowl created the circumstances that resulted in failed Midwestern (that is Oklahoma, Texas, Kansas, Nebraska, and parts of Colorado) farms, bank foreclosures, and desperate families migrating west. Regardless, most people can identify with the struggles of finding their own place in a new location or situation, especially the children of military personnel, workers routinely transferred by employers, and others who find that they must go where the jobs are. The unit could be expanded to include such books as Joan Bauer's *Hope Was Here* (2000), which narrates the difficulties and joys of one young woman who moves halfway across the United States with her aunt to start a new life.

A number of themes, concepts, and issues in *The Grapes of Wrath* can be developed through the picture books and the chapter books in this theme-set. In order to understand the Joads' migration from Sallisaw, Oklahoma to Bakersfield, California during the 1930s, students may use picture books and children's chapter books to learn about various kinds of migrant experiences, some of which students continue to experience today. The books in the theme-set baskets can be grouped into three general reading-level groups: the children's picture books, generally written for ages four to eight; the early and intermediate chapter books, written for ages nine to high school; and advanced books generally considered to be adult-level reading (a core text would fall into either of the last two categories, depending upon the grade level of the class). Poetry, videos, and nontraditional inclusions such as photographs, cartoons, and nonfiction articles may span all age groups.

> Collections of artifacts related to a book used for class reading or study . . . are sometimes called Jackdaws, which is actually a registered trademark of a company in Amawalk, NY that supplies collections of hands-on primary source artifacts [and] are available from the company at www.jackdaw.com, which offers archives of hands-on primary source documents by period, geographical location or interest. Teachers can begin with these collections or start with their own gleaned from garage sales, flea markets, eBay auctions, etc., but students should be encouraged to become active in adding to the collection, once they have begun reading a book. Such hunts for related items often involves families as students talk about the jackdaw at home, [where] parents and grandparents will also want to share their treasurers, some of which the children can take to class. Sometimes a speaker with first-hand knowledge can be invited to come in and bring in artifacts. (Strickland 2005, 90)

We have not specifically identified selections in the following list because teacher access to materials and student interest varies from class to class, and Internet and media articles can lose their timeliness. So, even after a theme-set basket is developed, selections may need to be modified from year to year.

THEME-SET BOOKS FOR MIGRANT FAMILIES

Core Literature

The Grapes of Wrath. Steinbeck, John. [1939] 1967. New York: Viking.

An Oklahoma farm family, the Joads, are driven off their homestead and forced to travel west to the promised land of California. The book follows the movements of thousands of other families as well and the consequent transformation of an entire nation.

Picture Books

A Day's Work. Bunting, Eve. 1994. New York: Clarion.

A small Mexican American boy, Francisco, acts as an interpreter for his grandfather, who just arrived in California and is looking for a job as a day laborer. The tense competition among the laborers in the yard demonstrates the desperation of people without work.

Amelia's Road. Altman, Linda Jacobs. 1993. New York: Lee and Low.

Amelia's family moves frequently to pick the crops. This time she particularly hates to move because she has been going to a school where, for the first time, the teacher has bothered to learn her name.

Calling the Doves. Herrera, Juan Felipe. 1995. Emeryville, CA: Children's Book Press.

In delightful and lyrical language, poet Juan Felipe Herrera tells the story of his migrant farmworker childhood in both English and Spanish. He recreates the joy of eating breakfast under the sky, listening to Mexican songs, and celebrating with other families at a fiesta in the mountains.

Gathering the Sun: An Alphabet in Spanish and English. Ada, Alma Flor. 1997. New York: Lothrop, Lee & Shepard.

Twenty-eight poems are offered in Spanish and English, celebrating everything from family to history to the bounty of the harvest. This collection takes the reader into the fields and the orchards as well as the lives of the people who work them.

Going Home. Bunting, Eve. 1996. New York: HarperCollins.

When Carlos and his family visit their home in Mexico, he begins to understand the sacrifices his parents have made, leaving loved ones behind to do brutally hard work so that their children can have better lives.

Lights on the River. Thomas, Jane Resh. 1994. New York: Hyperion.

A candle given to Teresa by her Mexican grandmother becomes a symbol of hope for her and her family as they struggle to survive as migrant laborers in America.

Tomas and the Library Lady. Mora, Pat. 1997. New York: Knopf.

While helping his family in their work as migrant laborers far from home, Tomas finds an entire world to explore in the books at the local public library. Based on the true story of the Mexican American author and educator, Tomas Rivera, this inspirational story suggests what libraries—and education—can make possible.

Working Cotton. Williams, Sherley Anne. 1992. New York: Harcourt Brace Jovanovich.

The author draws on her childhood experience in the cotton fields in Fresno for this evocative story of a migrant family's day. Shelan is too small to carry a bag, so she leaves her cotton in the rows for her mother to pick up. She admires her father because he picks cotton so fast she almost cannot see him do it, and she imagines how much cotton she could pick if she were as old as her sisters.

Chapter Books

A Migrant Family. Brimmer, Larry Dane. 1992. Minneapolis: Lerner.

Twelve-year-old Juan and his family are migrant workers from Mexico, who live near San Diego. Juan leads an uncertain, disjointed life, and while he is sometimes able to attend school, he has never known a permanent home. Black and white photography makes for an effective display of the hardships families like Juan's face.

Cesar Chavez: Hope for the People. Goodwin, David. 1991. New York: Ballantine.

The biography tells the story of Cesar Chavez as a young boy and a chronology of the struggle for building a movement to support better wages and working conditions for migrant workers.

The Circuit: Stories from the Life of a Migrant Child. Jimenez, Francisco. 1997. Albuquerque: New Mexico Press.

These eleven short stories, based on the author's experiences as a child in a migrant farmworker family, follow the family from leaving Mexico and entering the United States through years of moving from place to place, picking various crops, while trying to remain a loving family.

Y no se lo Traga la Tierra/ . . . And the Earth Did Not Devour Him. Rivera, Tomas. 1995. Houston, TX: Arte Publico.

A Mexican American family's life as migrant farmworkers during the 1950s is seen through the eyes of a young boy. Exploited by farmers, shopkeepers, and even fellow Mexican Americans, the boy must forge his identity in the face of death and disease, constant moving, and conflicts with school officials.

Young Adult Books

Children of the Dust Bowl: The True Story of the School at Weedpatch Camp. Stanley, Jerry. 1992. New York: Crown.

Told largely in the words of the migrants themselves, this photo essay is the compelling story of the "Okie" migration to California of the 1930s and of the remarkable school at a farmworkers' camp there. This book tells a story of prejudice being transformed into acceptance and despair into hope.

Dark Harvest: Migrant Farmworkers in America. Ashabranner, Brent. 1985. New York: Putnam Publishing Group Library.

Photographs and text show a true account of several families of migrant farmworkers in Texas and Florida.

Out of the Dust. Hesse, Karen. 1997. New York: Scholastic.

The author uses free verse to tell the story of a fourteen-year-old girl and her family's experiences trying to survive in the dust bowl of Oklahoma. Billie Jo is desperate to leave the dust even if it means she has to sacrifice everything she holds dear.

Voices from the Fields: Children of Migrant Farmworkers Tell Their Stories. Atkins, Beth. 1993. Boston: Little, Brown.

Interviews and photographs of nine Mexican American migrant youth tell the stories of their lives as migrant laborers, including their hopes, dreams, hardships, and obstacles. The nine stories are interspersed with Spanish and English poems, photographs, and statistics about the life of migrant workers.

High School—Adult

Rising in the West. Morgan, Dan. 1992. New York: Knopf.

Similar to Steinbeck's *Grapes of Wrath,* this story follows the family of one young man as he scrapes the money together for a battered old truck, gathers his desperate friends and family, and drives them to California. It illustrates the continuing hardships faced once families reached the far west and the struggles they encountered having to overcome the kinds of prejudice immigrants nearly always encounter.

The Plum Plum Pickers. Barrio, Raymond. 1984. New York: Bilingual Review Publishers.

The author depicts the life of an immigrant farmworker for whom poverty becomes a cycle caused by cold weather.

Who Will Know Us? New Poems. Soto, Gary. 1990. San Francisco: Chronicle.

A collection of poems divided into three sections. The first poem, "Red Palm," is the most appropriate in this collection on the theme of migrant families.

Related Books

Stolen Dreams: Portraits of Working Children. Parker, David L. 1998. Minneapolis: Lerner.

A photo-essay, this book tells the story of the approximately 250 million children around the world, including migrant farmworkers, who get up each day to go to work instead of to school. It is an honest and compassionate look at child labor in which readers will learn where and why children work and what can be done about the problems of child labor.

Theme-Set 1: | **23**
Migrant Families |

The Maldonado Miracle. Taylor, Theodore. 1973. New York: Avon.

Jose Maldonado has dreams of becoming an artist, but as the son of a poor Mexican farmer, he has to spend most of his time thinking about how to survive. In an attempt to be reunited with his father who had gone north to find work, Jose and his dog Sanchez find out what it's like to live in the world of the illegal alien. Hiding out in a church, Jose and Sanchez become the center of a "miracle" that finally reunites Jose with his father and gives him a new vision of a future where dreams can come true.

Working: People Talk About What They Do All Day and How They Feel About What They Do. Terkel, Studs. 1997. New York: New Press.

Terkel sat down with a grocery store clerk and a tape recorder and asked her about her job. She poured out her heart to him and the result is an intimate snapshot of one piece of the working lives of Americans. He proceeded to interview dozens of other people in various occupations, who create unique self-portraits of themselves at work.

USING *THE GRAPES OF WRATH* THEME-SET

The best mirrors of *The Grapes of Wrath* are *Out of the Dust* and *Children of the Dust Bowl* because of their setting and circumstances. Both books are young adult books with which the teacher could begin; however, the other young adult books in the bibliography are thematically linked as well. Not only do the books show the experiences of migrant workers during the Great Depression, but a number of picture books also depict the lives of migrant farmworkers in more recent times.

As explained in Chapter 2, students read the picture books, looking for common themes to discuss these in their small literacy circle group and with the whole class. When students move to the next set of books, they will see that similar themes also emerge. Students take turns reading one if not two of the young adult books for further discussions. We recommend using a compare-and-contrast chart that will guide the students as they read for common themes. Comparing and contrasting is a natural task that includes both recall and higher critical thinking skills.

Our students identified several thematic strands that add to the richness of the Migrant Families set: the struggle for an everyday existence, class conflict, and relationships forged among the families. We will briefly discuss each as examples of how picture books and young adult books scaffold students' understanding, allowing students to begin reading *The*

Grapes of Wrath with the background knowledge to make the book more interesting and approachable.

THE MIGRANT EXPERIENCE

In *The Grapes of Wrath*, the Joads are sharecroppers who had planted cotton for years in Oklahoma. However, when forced to leave their land and look for work elsewhere, they drive to California to pick seasonal crops such as grapes, peaches, and cotton. In *Working Cotton*, the pictures of beautiful oil paintings portray a day in the life of a Black family picking cotton from sunup to sundown. *Amelia's Road*, *Lights on the River*, and *Calling the Doves*, bring to mind a picture of individuals and families picking peaches, cucumbers, and apples. Within the beginning and intermediate-level chapter book category, the migrant experience is further explored. Brent Ashabranner's informational narrative in *Dark Harvest*, Larry Brimner's inside view of twelve-year-old Juan Medina in *A Migrant Family*, and Beth Atkin's interviews and photographs of nine migrant children in *Voices from the Fields* use nonfiction accounts to add to the picture. *Out of the Dust*, a book written in poetic form, tells of a family's experience with survival during the drought in Oklahoma. These books present several literary concepts and themes that will help students make intertextual connections between these books and the core selection. Three suggested by student literacy circle groups are (1) the struggle for an everyday existence, (2) class conflict, (3) relationships forged among the families.

The Struggle for an Everyday Existence

Many books in the set show the migrant routine of beginning work at dawn and finishing at dusk. In *Amelia's Road*, Amelia picks apples from dawn until she heads for school. In all the picture books, we see how the family works together as a unit. In *Lights on the River* and *Working Cotton*, the protagonists are girls who are not old enough to pick and, thus, are caretakers for the babies and the very young children in their families. In *Amelia's Road*, Amelia harvests carrots and lettuce alongside her parents. Migrant workers generally survive on a daily diet of staple foods such as rice and beans. Being able to afford meat, a more expensive food, for its protein value is important, especially to the families with growing children. When the Joads leave the government camp to pick cotton, they are able to earn more money to buy meat. Picking certain crops pays more money than others, which allows families to buy more than just the bare minimum. Occasionally, the mothers in *Lights on the River*, *Calling the Doves*, and in *Working Cotton* are also able to include meat.

Because migrant families are poor, relying on contractors to transport them or purchasing an old car is a common phenomenon. In *The Grapes of Wrath*, the Joads have a jalopy that breaks down and has to be fixed before continuing on their journey. By comparing *Working Cotton* with *Amelia's Road*, *Calling the Doves*, and *Lights on the River*, students can see the similarities and differences in forms of transportation farmworkers use to travel from one field to another. In *Working Cotton*, a bus transports the families to the cotton fields, and in the others each family relies on an old car to get them to work.

Migrants traveling to pick crops can neither afford a motel nor the deposit on rentals, which means that they must rely on any alternate type of shelter that is available. The Joads set up roadside camps and use the government camp at Weedpatch in Bakersfield, California. The picture books portray the various places where migrant families live. In *Amelia's Road*, the illustrations depict the numbered cabins in a labor camp; in *Lights on the River*, the author describes the makeshift houses they live in, including the chicken coop the Martinez family calls home while they pick peaches. In *Calling the Doves*, Herrera describes setting up a tent for the evening and later living in a ramshackle trailer his father built. Jimenez describes Tent City in *The Circuit*, rows of army tents that families set up for shelter while they pick strawberries. In Brimner's *A Migrant Family*, the migrant workers are not able to pay the $800 a month or more for rents in the area. The photographs illustrate the crude shacks made of orange or blue plastic sheets, plywood, and the trees used to support them outside Encinitas, California near San Diego.

Class Conflict

Many of the authors depict the tension between the property owners and the migrants. *A Migrant Family* discusses the conflicts that result when migrants set up shacks in the vicinity of expensive housing. Tension builds for the families that live in the red-tile roofed homes with security gates. These families complain to the health department about the danger of fire posed by the camp being so close to the trees and chaparral when it becomes dry. The health department is obligated to bring in bulldozers to eliminate the camp. Another example of this tension occurs when Teresa Martinez in *Lights on the River* returns the bowl that the farmer's wife had brought over containing fruit and milk. Teresa gets a firsthand look at the luxuries the farmer's family experiences and compares them to her own. Steinbeck depicts a similar conflict: The landowners worry about their property and protect themselves by burning the camps where there exists any tension between the grower and the laborers; they also form armed squads of clerks and local workers.

Relationships Forged Among the Migrant Families

Having lived among the Oklahoma Okies, Steinbeck depicts the human interactions and bonds that were forged under such dire financial hardships. For example, the Wilsons share their quilt and tear a page from their Bible, offering it to the Joads when Grandpa dies; in return Al Joad fixes their car. A number of theme-set books also portray examples of helping others. In *The Circuit*, Lupe Gordillo, from a nearby labor camp, brings the Jimenez family a few groceries and introduces the family to the camp foreman.

Parallels can be drawn between characters in *The Grapes of Wrath* and real-life migrant workers as well. Casy, the ex-preacher who struggles with the ideas of God, holiness, and sin in organized religion, comes to his own understanding of these concepts. Toward the end of the novel, Casy becomes a spokesperson and leader for the migrant workers who have been deceived by the Hopper Ranch owner who had promised to pay workers five cents a box but instead pays them half that amount. With Casy's help, the migrant workers organize a strike at the ranch. In the 1960s, Cesar Chavez became a leader and championed the rights of farm workers by creating a union that would join together workers to gain better working conditions. In Goodwin's *Cesar Chavez: Hope for the People*, the author describes the tensions between the growers and the farmworkers and the events that led Cesar Chavez to create a farmworkers' union.

Language

Another important consideration in many of the texts is the language used. Although the authentic word choice of the authors is not in itself a theme, it is a common factor that derives from geographical location, class, and sometimes, ethnicity. The southern vernacular used in *The Grapes of Wrath* conversations is an important feature that carries the reader into the lives of the Joads and other Okies migrating west. One of the phonological features of the southern rural dialect reduces -ing to -in' in verbs such as *fishin'* and *goin'*. One common lexical feature is the frequent use of *ain't*, which is a nonstandard contraction for "am not" in Standard English usage. As for the syntactical features, the southern rural dialect makes much more frequent use of the double negative than does the Standard, as in "there ain't nobody can tell you different" (Steinbeck [1939] 1967, 43).

Other authors such as Jimenez in *The Circuit* and Rivera in *And the Earth Did Not Devour Him* sprinkle the narratives with Spanish. In Atkin's book, too, several of the migrant youth use Spanish words to talk about their experiences as migrants (1993).

ACTIVITIES USING MULTIPLE INTELLIGENCES

Activities revolving around the theme-sets may draw upon all the intelligences learners possess (Gardner 1983, 1993). Dignifying the artistic response to literature may provide a means for experiencing what it means for a reader to enter, create, and participate in a story world, especially for readers who may not naturally see and experience what they read, whether because of operative reading difficulties or because of limited language proficiency. Visual response is a very democratic form of response not only because it is useful in different ways to different students but also because it validates a form of knowing and exploring not frequently considered in the secondary classroom. Art, unlike more traditional forms of linguistic response, is not perceived by students as being "correct" or "incorrect." It may, therefore, open doors for readers who have become resistant to contributing in class because they have so often gotten the impression from the teacher or classmates that they are wrong or because their response has been devalued in some way. Artistic response encourages risk taking because it is more open to interpretation than the answers to authority-generated questions about a reading, and it promotes higher-level thinking because it requires explanation and application. The following activities have been designed to maximize success for all students. To assist students in their reading in the theme-set, a teacher might provide a map of old Route 66. Although the activities listed below may be done by individuals after adaptations, they are best completed within a group. Students will be working toward exploration of the themes in a multigenre mode as well as within Gardner's multiple intelligences (1983, 1993). Each activity has been designed to be completed while the groups are "traveling" on Route 66 from Oklahoma to California, and though there are no specific sites, they are representative of places migrants might have worked or experienced during the Dust Bowl years. Many experiences are apropos to today's migrant workers as well. As a last note, due to space limitations, Milepost 1 is the only one that is detailed. All others are merely listed.

Milepost 1

Leaving a place that is the only refuge you have ever known can be traumatic. However, when you lose your home, personal items can represent "home" to you. In *Going Home*, Carlos' parents revisit their longtime home in Mexico with him in tow. He sees his parents' emotional reacquaintance with their long-ago residence. The Joad family has to experience leaving a longtime family home as well.

Individually, visualize your home. You are going to make selections of items that you simply could not leave behind if you had to leave everything else in a household move, as the Joads and Carlos' parents had to do.

1. Select one item that most represents your family. Then select an item your family uses the most. Next, choose the one item that your family is most proud of. Finally, select an item that you think has the most value to your parent(s), or grandparent(s), or any other caretakers with whom you live.
2. In writing, explain the reason behind each choice.
3. Design and then actually create a container that will hold the items so they may be safely transported. Create a symbolic or realistic representation of the items. Place those items in your container.
4. Discuss with your group how you think the family in *The Grapes of Wrath* feels in making the selection of items that had to be left behind. (Linguistic, Spatial, Interpersonal, Logical-Mathematical)

Milepost 2

Using *Out of the Dust*, focus on the experience of watching the dust overtake the family farm, an experience the Joads know all too well. Use this discussion focus starter: "The Joad family is like the Kirby family because, like the Kirby family, they _____" and two other statements of similar comparison. Justify each family's way of dealing with life. (Linguistic, Logical-Mathematical)

Milepost 3

In *Dark Harvest*, Chapter 2, or in *The Circuit*, the change of seasons is the natural force that determines people's way of living. Yet, the families were able to deal with nature by moving around. There is a pattern to their survival techniques. In graphic form, create a map that details the track the migrants need to follow to continue working season by season. (Spatial, Logical-Mathematical, Naturalist)

Milepost 4

We remember the pictures of the migrant workers that Dorothea Lange took in Nipomo, California. Use the Internet and *Children of the Dust Bowl* to research pictures of the Dust Bowl immigrants. In your literacy circle groups, create a word bank that describes what you see in the pictures. Categorize the words into logical groups and use those groups to recaption the pictures. (Linguistic, Spatial, Naturalist)

Milepost 5

To give you some background, go to the following websites to listen to MIDI music of the 1930s and read some background on the music

> http://blues.about.com/cs/songcollections
> www.bozeman.k12.mt.us/bhslib/music.html.

After you have read the information and listened to the sample of the music, capture the flavor of the 1930s by creating the lyrics to a song that any of the characters in one of the Dust Bowl era books would have sung. (Musical, Linguistic, Logical-Mathematical)

Milepost 6

Compare children's views in *Voices from the Fields* or *The Circuit* or *A Migrant Family* with the children's views of the experience in *The Grapes of Wrath*. (Linguistic)

Milepost 7

Read Gary Soto's poem "Red Palm" in the book, *Who Will Know Us?* This poem shows Soto getting into the minds of the field-workers. Use this as inspiration to create a poetic retelling of Pa Joad's desperation as the family fortunes continue to fall. (Linguistic, Spatial)

Milepost 8

The landowners and the big agricultural businesses in *The Grapes of Wrath* and a number of other books in the set fear the migrant workers' solidarity will force them to pay higher wages for labor that will, in turn, drive down their profits. Intense hunger and need unite all the migrants in their common misery. In a choral reading, demonstrate a scene where this problem is evident. (Linguistic, Interpersonal, Bodily-Kinesthetic)

Milepost 9

Living conditions are usually primitive for migrants. Using what you read in *The Grapes of Wrath*, *The Circuit*, *Lights on the River*, *Calling the Doves*, *Amelia's Road*, and *Children of the Dust Bowl*, create a poster board scene of migrant housing or more generally the migrant experience. Then create an original caption for the poster board and go to a scene in the book or source and select two quotes for the poster. Prepare the product for a "gallery walk," in which all posters will be displayed.

Note for this milepost: The poster board scene is an activity that can be assigned as a group task, allowing English learners the opportunity for interacting with others using academic language common in the language arts or English classroom. Literacy circles of four work well. As a group of four, each is responsible for contributing equally (each member is designated a particular color marker). The equitable participation can be further reinforced as part of the criteria given as part of the assignment. It can be further reinforced if the criteria is spelled out in a written rubric.

The gallery walk, too, is an activity that promotes high levels of language development for English learners with threshold levels of English (intermediate level and above). English learners can participate in the gallery walk by listening to others explain their poster or, if brave enough, can be the docent explaining the poster to others. Two literacy circle members need to be designated as docents to detail the scene on the poster board while others take the "walk" to see the posters produced by other groups. The first docent explains the poster then switches off with the second docent after half of the designated time for the walk has passed so that the first gets a turn at the gallery walk. (Spatial, Linguistic, Bodily-Kinesthetic)

Milepost 10

In many of the books, such as *The Circuit* and *Amelia's Road*, the children dread having to leave their school friends every time they migrate to the next work site. Using a Socratic Seminar, join the class in discussing the following statements.

1. The only way out of poverty is to gain an education.
2. People who share a common direction and a sense of community can get where they are going quicker because they are traveling on each other's trust.
3. "Even if I knew the world would go to pieces tomorrow, I would still plant my apple tree."—Martin Luther King (Linguistic)

Milepost 11

Using several of the books in the theme-set basket as well as *The Grapes of Wrath*, make a list of various aspects of life that migrant families have in common (for example, transportation and family loyalty). Categorize the words. For each category, create four true statements. Each person in the literacy circle must choose any one of the true statements to use as a caption on unlined paper. This paper will become the cover to a short reflective essay that connects their chosen statement to the books read for the assignment. (Spatial, Linguistic)

Milepost 12

In all the books you have read, you have gained a clear picture of life for American migrants. Using the categories of Food, Transportation, Hard Work, Living Conditions, Diversions, and Seasons (and other categories that the groups thought of in Milepost 11), accurately describe the life of a migrant. You must use quotations, pictures, examples, and maps or graphics. Create a Migrant Life Box, a container that holds symbolic or accurate representations of a group of persons sharing common experiences, in which you place the evidence of your description. On the outside of the box, post your own one-sentence statement on migrant life. (Linguistic, Spatial, Intrapersonal, Logical-Mathematical, Bodily-Kinesthetic)

These activities emphasize theme, connect texts, offer student choice, and provide opportunities for students of various intelligence strengths to shine while taking into consideration the needs of our English language learners. A summative assessment may be designed around the Milepost Activities—perhaps a portfolio of student-chosen work. Most teachers will still wish to incorporate a more traditional unit paper-and-pen test or a linguistic assessment such as an expository paper. In combination, these assessments will provide powerful insight into the students' understanding of the texts and the themes through which they have just navigated.

4 | THEME-SET 2: GROWING UP ETHNIC IN AMERICA— THE AFRICAN AMERICAN EXPERIENCE

Core Text: Their Eyes Were Watching God *by Zora Neale Hurston*

We want our students to be comfortable with diversity, and one important way to accomplish this is to read ethnic and racial literature from an informed perspective. Reading the literature and history of African Americans helps students to see how people of that ethnic background have contributed to the larger American society. The core text we selected for the Growing Up Ethnic in America—The African American Experience theme-set is Zora Neale Hurston's *Their Eyes Were Watching God* (1978), which tells the story of the maturing of Janie Mae Crawford, a beautiful young black woman in racially segregated Florida. The novel was first published in 1937, but it contains timeless themes that are of interest to young adults today: growing up, relationships, marriage, beauty, and racial, biracial, and ethnic identity.

Growing Up Ethnic in America—The African American Experience, a variation of the coming-of-age theme, is a rich one that teachers can mold to fit their regional needs, organizing the theme-set around the African American experience. The teacher may also choose to add other cultural groups to diversify the theme of Growing Up Ethnic in America—The African American Experience. The other groups chosen may be represented in the school and the surrounding community, or they may be peoples with whom the students do not ordinarily interact. We recommend choosing multiethnic literature that represents the following cultural groups: Asian Americans, Pacific Islanders, Hispanic Americans, and Native Americans. Because multicultural literature reinforces and dignifies individual and group experiences, it acts as both a mirror for minority students' own lives and a window for majority students' learning about others. In other words, it is for *all* students.

Much has been written about the inclusion of African Americans in the academic literature on multiculturalism (Banks 1995; Garcia 2001; Nieto 1999; Palumbo-Liu 1995; Sleeter and Grant 1999). African American history has either been omitted or told erroneously in many history books. Moreover, African Americans have often been viewed stereotypically. For a review of stereotypes of various races and ethnicities, view the website www.authentichistory.com/diversity/. One thinks, for example, of African Americans being treated as comical or violent. These stereotypes have usually been created by authors who neither were part of the culture they depicted, nor spent much time researching them. Today, on the other hand, cultural authenticity has become an important criterion in multicultural literature (Sims Bishop 1997).

From 1900 to 1950, publications by African Americans in music, art, and literature in New York City, especially in Harlem, surged. Blacks from Africa and the Caribbean, as well as other parts of the United States, moved to New York in pursuit of economic prosperity and social equality while dreaming of contributing to the American artistic and literary canon. Zora Neale Hurston moved to New York from Florida in 1925, received a B.A. degree in 1928 from Barnard College (the female affiliate of Columbia University), and began to write plays and novels in 1932. Other African American writers active at this time in New York included W. E. B. DuBois, Ralph Ellison, Jessie Faust, Langston Hughes, Alain Locke, Dorothy West, and Richard Wright. The literary works of these Harlem Renaissance writers influenced current authors, such as Toni Morrison, Gloria Naylor, and Alice Walker.

In 1950, Gwendolyn Brooks received a Pulitzer Prize for her book of poetry *Annie Allen* (1949). In 1952, Ralph Ellison won the National Book Award for his novel *The Invisible Man* ([1947] 1980), and James Baldwin's *Go Tell It on the Mountain* was published soon after ([1952] 1980). In 1960, Lorraine Hansberry's *A Raisin in the Sun* ([1959] 1966) won the New York Drama Critics' Circle Award and was the first play by an African American woman to ever be produced on Broadway. Five years later, *The Autobiography of Malcolm X* (1965) was a best seller, and Maya Angelou's memoir *I Know Why the Caged Bird Sings* was published in 1969.

From the 1970s to the present day, many first-rate works by African American authors have been published, including Alex Haley's novel *Roots* (1976), which became a TV drama in 1977; Toni Morrison's novels, *Song of Solomon* (1977) and *Beloved* (1987), for which she received the Nobel Prize for Literature in 1993; Alice Walker's, *The Color Purple* (1982), which was later adapted into a movie (1985) by director Steven Spielberg; and August Wilson's plays, *Fences* (1995) and *The Piano Lesson* (1990), for which he won the Pulitzer Prize in 1986 and 1990, respectively.

Many African American authors have written for children and young adults, especially since the 1960s. Notable among these authors are: Virginia Hamilton (*Zeely*, 1986); Walter Dean Myers (*Scorpions*, 1988); Mildred Taylor (*Roll of Thunder*, 1976); and Tom Feelings (*Middle Passage*, 1995). The next generation of writers included: Patricia McKissick (*Young, Black and Determined: A Biography of Lorraine Hansberry*, 1998); Cindy Dawson Boyd (*Fall Secrets*, 1994); and Sharon Bell Mathis (*The Hundred Penny Box*, 1975). These authors wrote books with universal themes through the perspective of the African American experience. A more recent generation of African American writers for children and young adults has included: Jacqueline Woodson (*Last Summer with Maizon*, 1990); Christopher Paul Curtis (*The Watsons Go to Birmingham— 1963*, 1995); and Rita Williams-Garcia (*Blue Tights*, 1988).

Some of the most widely recognized African American authors of picture books are Donald Crews (*Bigmama's*, 1991), Elizabeth Fitzgerald Howard (*Aunt Flossie's Hats*, 1991), Eloise Greenfield (*Honey, I Love and Other Love Poems*, 1978), Julius Lester (*From Slave Ship to Freedom Road*, 1998), Robert D. San Souci (*The Talking Eggs*, 1989), and Faith Ringgold (*Tar Beach*, 1991). A good number of these authors have received the Coretta Scott King Author Book Award, which is presented annually to an African American author for his or her outstanding contributions to children's literature. Working alongside the picture book authors are African American illustrators of note: Pat Cummings (in *Good News: Formerly "Bubbles"* by Eloise Greenfield, 1977), Leo and Diane Dillon (in *Her Stories* by Virginia Hamilton, 1995), Tom Feelings (*Middle Passage: White Ships/Black Cargo*, 1995), Jan Spivey Gilchrist (in *Kia Tanisha Drives Her Car* by Eloise Greenfield, 1997), Brian Pinkney (in *The Dark Thirty: Southern Tales of the Supernatural* by Patricia McKissack, 1992), Jerry Pinkney (in *The Talking Eggs* by Robert San Souci, 1989), and James Ransome (in *Aunt Flossie's Hats* by Elizabeth Fitzgerald Howard, 1991), all of whom have been recipients of the Coretta Scott King Illustrator Award, the illustrator equivalent to the Author Book Award.

A handy resource that provides brief biographical sketches and book titles for ethnic authors writing for young adults and children is Frances Ann Day's *Multicultural Voices in Contemporary Literature: A Resource for Teachers* (1999).

Because we advocate using multiethnic literature as part of the theme-set, it is important for teachers to be familiar with the broader multicultural themes found in ethnic literature. Multicultural literature is an important component of multicultural education because it provides readers with the vicarious experiences of groups that are outside the sociopolitical mainstream. Multicultural education rejects racism and other forms of prejudice, embracing instead the notion of a pluralistic society in which people of all ages, ethnicities, races, religions, cultures, economic statuses, and sexual orientations are equal (Banks 1995; Nieto 1999). Some of the salient themes that distinguish multicultural from mainstream texts include:

- leaving behind one's homeland (voluntarily or involuntarily)
- being oppressed and defeated by discrimination
- surviving discrimination with dignity
- telling the historical and cultural roots of social groups
- living day to day with heritage values, attitudes, behaviors, religious beliefs
- fitting into two worlds
- organizing for social justice
- promoting cultural renewal in the arts

Teachers can relate these broader themes to the African American experience. For example, for the first theme, leaving behind one's homeland, the class can discuss the differences between the African diaspora spurred by the slave trade and European immigration impelled by religious persecution and poverty.

The recommended books from this theme-set that support this theme are Tom Feeling's *Middle Passage: White Ship/Black Cargo* (1995), Julius Lester's *From Slave Ship to Freedom Road* (1998), Dorothy Hoobler's and Thomas Hoobler's *The African American Family Album* (1995), Faith Ringgold's *Aunt Harriet's Underground Railroad in the Sky* (1992), and Frederick Douglass' *Narrative of the Life of Frederick Douglass: An American Slave* ([1845] 1999).

To organize and present this multicultural theme-set successfully, teachers should prepare their students for reading novels with multicultural themes by first introducing the general historical context of African Americans. It is difficult to understand multicultural themes without knowing their historical context.

The historical background of African Americans in the United States is tied to the founding and expansion period of this nation. Agriculture became profitable because of the low-cost physical labor performed by slaves. Between 1741 and 1760, importation of slaves was at its peak, which allowed plantation owners to prosper, producing tobacco in Virginia, rice and indigo in the Carolinas, wheat in Maryland, and cotton throughout the South. Although there is a long history of rebellion and resistance to slavery by the slaves themselves and some whites, especially the Quakers, the abolitionist movement attracted many whites, especially between 1830 and 1859. Nat Turner led seventy fellow slaves in a major rebellion in Southampton, Virginia, in 1831, and William Lloyd Garrison formed the New England Anti-Slavery Society the following year. Frederick Douglass gave his first antislavery speech in Nantucket, Massachusetts in 1841; and in 1849, Harriet Tubman began the Underground Railroad, the hidden network of people and places that allowed slaves to escape the United States with their freedom into Canada. Harriet Beecher Stowe's novel *Uncle Tom's Cabin* ([1851] 1964) gained wide attention for the abolitionist cause.

Over the course of the next fifty years, the Civil War unfolded (1861–1865), the Emancipation Proclamation freed the slaves in the Confederate States (1863), slavery was abolished by the Thirteenth Amendment (1865), full civil liberties were granted by the Fourteenth Amendment (1868), but the Supreme Court ruled in *Plessey v. Ferguson* that "separate but equal" was constitutional (1896), which spurred many Jim Crow laws. From 1900 to 1930, the years of the so-called New Negro Movement, many African Americans moved to northern states from the South to pursue social and economic opportunities. During the 1930s, the Great Depression affected everyone, especially African Americans. From 1940 to 1969, activism among African Americans to gain full legal equality with whites gained momentum, resulting in the civil rights legislation of the 1960s.

Instructors should be aware that teaching multicultural literature is not without its difficulties, as we saw in Cherry Hill, New Jersey, in 1995. At that time, a controversy arose when an English teacher began a unit on Mark Twain's *The Adventures of Huckleberry Finn* ([1884] 1948) without first informing her eleventh graders that the novel had controversial content and that the word *nigger* appeared some two hundred times in the book. The result was that the African American students became self-conscious whenever the N word was read aloud, and the white students would turn around to stare or snicker. African American parents protested to the administration. The issue was eventually resolved when it turned out that no one wanted to have the book banned. Rather, they wanted it to be studied in its full historical context. After this decision, any teacher in Cherry Hill who wished to teach *Huckleberry Finn* first had to take a one-day workshop on the novel's historical context at a nearby university. (For a review of the entire controversy, see www.pbs.org/wgbh/cultureshock/teachers/huck/controversy.html.)

THE STORY OF ZORA NEALE HURSTON'S
THEIR EYES WERE WATCHING GOD

Hurston's novel revolves around the life of Janie Mae Crawford, a beautiful, fair-skinned, seventeen-year-old African American girl living in western rural Florida in the early twentieth century. Janie's grandmother, Nanny, convinces the girl to marry Logan Killicks, who is at least twenty years older than Janie but provides financial stability in the form of a 60-acre farm. As time passes and the novelty of the marriage wears off, Logan wants Janie to work side by side with him as he plants crops and takes care of the farm animals. Janie has never done any physical labor harder than housework, and has no interest in shoveling horse manure, milking cows, or plowing fields.

When Logan goes off to buy a mule, Janie meets Joe Stark, who is taken with her beauty and invites her to run off with him. She shouldn't be doing hard farm work, he says. As *his* woman, all she'll have to do is make his meals, sit out on the porch, and look pretty.

When Logan returns with the mule, he orders Janie to clean up the manure, which inspires her to decide that the time is ripe to run off with Joe, who takes her to a minister in town and marries her on the spot. The couple head for Eatonville, an all-black town in south Florida, where Joe has plans to turn the town into a black paradise without racial discrimination. He and Janie open a general store, and during its grand opening Joe is elected mayor of the town. The porch on the front of the store is eventually where all the people in town come to tell stories. This gives the author, who had studied under the famous anthropologist Franz Boaz at Columbia University, a chance to insert folkstories into her narrative. Most of the people come to tell or listen to stories, although some of the men come to look at gorgeous Janie.

Everything goes well for the next fifteen years until Joe dies of kidney failure. Nine months later, Janie meets a laborer and gambler named Tea Cake, and the two of them hit it off right away. Before long, they're heading for the Everglades, where Tea Cake eventually lands a job cutting sugar cane and picking green beans. Because Janie loves him so much, she works right beside him in the fields, something she never would have done with Logan Killicks.

Unfortunately, during a flood, Tea Cake is bitten by a vicious dog and soon dies of rabies. Left on her own, the thirty-five-year-old Janie returns to Eatonville, a far more mature and independent woman than ever before.

GROWING UP ETHNIC IN AMERICA—THE AFRICAN AMERICAN EXPERIENCE THEME-SET

Core Literature

Their Eyes Were Watching God. Hurston, Zora Neale. 1978. Urbana: University of Illinois Press.

Janie Mae Crawford's life in rural Florida, surviving three husbands and the trials of womanhood.

Picture Books

A Place Called Freedom. Sanders, Scott Russell. 1997. New York: Simon & Schuster.

In 1832, when the narrator, James, is seven years old, his family is freed by their kindhearted slave master in Tennessee, who gives them money and urges them to seek freedom in a northern state. James' father, Joshua, leads the family to Indiana, traveling only at night, following the North Star, to avoid whites who might re-enslave them. When they finally get to Indiana, Joshua changes the family name to Starman because of his love of stars. Some Quakers take the family in and loan them seeds, a mule, and a plow. Soon they have earned enough money to buy their own land and build a humble cabin on it. Joshua then makes several trips back to Tennessee to lead his sisters and brothers and their families to join him on the farm. Eventually, the farm grows into a town, which they name Freedom. The story is based on true events that occurred in Tennessee and Lyles Station, Indiana. For more information, go to http://princeton-indiana.com/pages/history/lyles-Station.htm.

Aunt Flossie's Hats (and Crab Cakes Later). Howard, Elizabeth Fitzgerald. 1991. New York: Clarion House.

Susan and her sister, Sarah, are enthralled by their great-great-aunt Flossie's hatboxes. As the girls look in each box, Aunt Flossie tells them the story behind the hat. The stories range from a great fire in Baltimore that she witnessed, to big parades that she attended, to Sunday outings that she went on as a young girl with her family. James Ransome has illustrated the book with beautiful paintings.

Aunt Harriet's Underground Railroad in the Sky. Ringgold, Faith. 1992. New York: Crown.

In this story, illustrated by the author with paintings, Cassie Louise Lightfoot is flying in the sky when she comes upon the Underground Railroad, depicted here as a literal flying train. The next thing we know, Cassie is one of the slaves on the train, and we see through her eyes how slaves escaped to freedom. First, they were hidden in homes by sympathetic whites and free blacks and then transported through graveyards and secret compartments of hearses until they reached freedom in Canada. Cassie's story is followed by a brief biography of Harriet Tubman, the main "conductor" of the Underground Railroad.

From Slave Ship to Freedom Road. Based on Paintings by Rod Brown. Lester, Julius. 1998. New York: Dial.

In this book, the reader is invited to imagine the horror of slavery and the resiliency of the slaves by viewing twenty-one of Rod Brown's paintings that have been exhibited in museums under the title *From Slavery to Freedom*. The first set of paintings depicts the beginning of the slave trade as the chained slaves are transported on ships and sold as property. Domestic slaves work in homes, washing clothes and caring for children, while field slaves work on plantations, picking cotton, tobacco, or wheat. The second set of paintings depicts the maltreatment of slaves, including the punishment of runaways and the separation of children from their mothers. The third and final set of paintings depicts the liberation of the slaves, including scenes of the Underground Railroad, black soldiers fighting in the Civil War, and the formal announcement by military personnel that the slaves have been freed. Exercises are scattered throughout the book, inviting readers to imagine themselves as victims and aggressors in various historical circumstances.

I Have a Dream. King, Dr. Martin Luther. [1968] 1999. New York: Scholastic.

Dr. King's well-known speech was given on August 28, 1963, in Washington, D.C., before 250,000 people. The speech is beautifully illustrated in this book by fifteen renowned artists, including Leo and Diane Dillon, Tom Feelings, Brian Pinkney, Jerry Pinkney, Jan Spivey Gilchrist, and James Ransome. Each illustration corresponds to a different section of the speech.

Mufaro's Beautiful Daughters. Steptoe, John. 1987. New York: Lothrop, Lee & Shepard.

An African tale about two beautiful teenage girls, Manyara and Nyasha, is a study in characters with contrasting personalities. Manyara is vain and selfish while Nyasha is humble and generous. After the king announces that he wishes to marry the worthiest and most beautiful woman in the land, Manyara sets out early in order to be the first to meet him. The story ends with a twist that sets it apart from other Cinderella stories.

Tar Beach. Ringgold, Faith. 1991. New York: Crown.

Illustrated with photographs of quilts made by the author herself, this is the story of an eight-year-old heroine, Cassie Louise Lightfoot, who dreams of being free to go wherever she wants. She flies over the rooftop of her home, looking down at her family, sails over the George Washington Bridge to Manhattan, and on to the union hall that her father helped to build. In a note at the end, the author describes how her art combines storytelling, quilting, and the African American theme of flying as a metaphor for escaping slavery. African American women quilting dates back to the days of slavery and the quilters incorporated African American motifs.

The Faithful Friend. San Souci, Robert. 1995. New York: Simon & Schuster Books for Young Readers.

This is a beautifully illustrated tale of romance set in the late nineteenth century on the island of Martinique in the Caribbean. Two young men who are close friends, Clement and Hippolyte, have grown up together on a sugar plantation owned by Clement's father. Clement and Hippolyte set out to meet the beautiful Pauline Zabocat, whom Clement wants to marry. However, her uncle, Monsieur Zabocat, opposes this, preferring that his niece marry a wealthy gentleman from France. When Clement and Pauline run away together, Monsieur Zabocat hires three women to kill the couple, but Hippolyte foils the plot. The story has its roots in the "Faithful John" tales by the brothers Grimm, but with distinctively West Indian characters and other features.

The Talking Eggs. San Souci, Robert. 1989. New York: Dial Books for Young Readers.

This Cinderella-type folktale uses beautiful illustrations to tell the story of two sisters: Rose, the older sister, is spoiled and lazy, whereas Blanche, the younger one, is sweet but forced to do all the heavy work around the house because Rose is the mother's favorite. One day, Blanche meets an old woman who invites her to her home but makes Blanche promise that she will not laugh at her. When they get to the cottage, Blanche discovers crazy-colored chickens and other odd creatures in the barn, and when she sits down at the kitchen table for tea, the old lady takes off her own head and holds it in her lap. Nevertheless, Blanche keeps her promise not to laugh. The old lady then rewards her by telling her to go out to the barn and take eggs from the chickens. The old lady instructs Blanche to take the plain ones and throw them over her shoulder as she walks home. When Blanche follows these instructions, fine clothes and a carriage appear, and she returns home in splendor. Her mother then sends Rose into the woods to meet the old woman, and she, too, is invited to the old woman's cottage. Rose laughs and disobeys the old lady; when she throws the eggs over her shoulder, they turn into snakes, toads, yellow jackets, and a big gray spiders, which chase her home. This is a Creole folktale with roots in the European fairy tales.

Uncle Jed's Barbershop. Mitchell, Margaree King. 1993. New York: Simon & Schuster.

Uncle Jed's dream of owning a barbershop is told by his niece, Sarah Jean, who begins the story when she was six years old, and he was her favorite uncle. Jed earns money by cutting people's hair in their homes, so he is always hoping to get his own shop. Unfortunately, his dream is delayed twice. The first time, Sarah Jean needs an operation, and Uncle Jed pays for it. The second time, he loses his money when his bank goes broke during the Great Depression. Jed finally makes his dream come true when he is eighty-nine, a lesson in determination for everyone.

Working Cotton. Williams, Sherley Anne. 1992. New York: Harcourt Brace Jovanovich.

The author draws on her childhood experience in the cotton fields near Fresno, California for this evocative story of a day in the life of a migrant family. The young heroine, Shelan, is too small to carry a bag, so she leaves her cotton in the rows for her mother to pick up. She admires her father because he picks cotton so fast that she almost can't see him do it. She also imagines how much cotton she could pick if she were as old as her sisters. Williams wrote the preface to Zora Neale Hurston's *Their Eyes Were Watching God*.

Zora Neale Hurston, Writer and Storyteller. McKissack, Patricia. 1991. New York: Enslow.

This is an illustrated biography of Zora Neale Hurston that traces her life as a Harlem Renaissance writer, folklorist, and anthropologist. She sought to preserve the storytelling traditions of African Americans by publishing these stories in her novels.

Young Adult Books

Cousins. Hamilton, Virginia. 1990. New York: Philomel.

This story is told by an eleven-year-old girl, Cammy, who describes her friendship with two of her cousins: Elodie, who is plain, and Patty Ann, who is beautiful. Although all three girls are the same age, Cammy gets along well with Elodie, who tends to follow her lead, but constantly fights with Patty Ann, who is the darling of their school. One hot summer day, the camp program in which the three cousins are enrolled takes the children to Little River State Park. When the girls prepare to walk into the river, one of Elodie's shoes accidentally falls into the water. As Elodie tries to retrieves it, she is swept away by the current. Patty Ann rushes in to save her but drowns. Cammy is so sad and depressed that she is unable to sleep alone and constantly blames herself for the accident. A special visit by her ninety-four-year-old grandmother helps her to cope with the tragic loss of her cousin.

Middle Passage: White Ships/Black Cargo. Feelings, Tom. 1995. New York: Dial.

This book tells its story—the Atlantic slave trade—totally in pictures. Feelings researched and painted sixty-four black-and-white line drawings of the horrific experience. In a preface, the historian John Henrick Clarke provides an overview of the middle passage—that is, the second leg of the triangular trade route from Europe to Africa to the New World. Enduring the middle passage required extreme physical strength, mental tenacity, and spiritual determination for five to twelve weeks that these drawings depict. Captives were shackled in pairs, confined in a prone position in the dark lower deck of the ship. Although the slave trade was a lucrative economic system, it had its perils, for the slaves sometimes rose up and killed the captain and the crew.

Roll of Thunder, Hear My Cry. Taylor, Mildred D. 1976. New York: Dial.

This story is set in Mississippi in the 1930s when Jim Crow laws were in effect. Nine-year-old Cassie Logan lives with her parents and three brothers, growing cotton on their 400-acre farm. In addition, the mother, Mrs. Logan, is the seventh-grade teacher at the local all-black Great Faith Elementary School, which Cassie and her brothers attend. Because of the low price of cotton at the time, Cassie's parents have to supplement their income to pay their property taxes. Mr. Logan finds work in Louisiana laying train tracks. Cassie narrates the events of her life during her father's absence, describing the terrible impact the "separate but equal" Jim Crow laws have on her family.

The African American Family Album. Hoobler, Dorothy, and Thomas Hoobler. 1995. New York: Oxford University Press.

This book is a collection of memories and experiences of Africans and African Americans. It has six chapters that focus on the history of African Americans, beginning with a chapter on their homeland, life in Africa. The subsequent chapters include the following topics: the middle passage, slavery, a new life under the Jim Crow laws, the migration from south to north, and the Civil Rights movement.

The Friendship. Taylor, Mildred D. 1987. New York: Dial Books for Young Readers.

A short story about Tom Bee, an African American man, who saves John Wallace, a European American fifteen-year-old teenager, from drowning in a swamp, and moreover, Tom Bee cares for John until he is over a bout with a fever. A friendship is forged and before John goes away he promises to always have Tom Bee call him "John." After a number of years John returns and opens up a general store. During this time period, African Americans are to address all whites by using "Mr." or "Mrs." and their full name. When Tom Bee enters John's general store he addresses him as "John." The other white neighbors and John Wallace's grown sons are incensed by what they believe to be disrespect of a black man toward a white man. Because the two grown sons are so disrespectful of Tom Bee, he prefers to talk directly with John. The friendship is strained and a terrible thing happens when Tom Bee continues to call John by his first name in front of other white men.

The Gold Cadillac. Taylor, Mildred D. 1987. New York: Dial Books for Young Readers.

Lois and Wilma's father buys a brand new 1950 gold Cadillac. Unfortunately, it becomes the center of conflict between the father and mother because, instead of saving money for a new house, the father has purchased a luxury car. Further conflict ensues when the father decides to visit his parents in Mississippi. The mother as well as the uncles and aunts see the danger of a black man driving a gold Cadillac in the South, and they all decide to go with him. They caravan through Ohio and Tennessee, but in traffic the three families become separated. The father is arrested and taken to jail because the two policeman do not believe that he is the owner of the gold Cadillac. After a night of sleeping in the car before driving into Mississippi, the father decides that he cannot risk his family's life, and so he trades his car with a cousin living in Tennessee. The family reaches Mississippi and spends a week visiting. They return to Tennessee, trade cars with the cousin, and leave for Ohio in their gold Cadillac. Immediately afterward, the father sells the Cadillac. This is a story from Mildred Taylor's life.

The People Could Fly. Hamilton, Virginia. 1986. New York: Knopf.

This is a collection of twenty-four folktales divided into four categories by theme: (1) animal tales; (2) extravagant and fanciful tales; (3) supernatural tales; and (4) slave tales of freedom. The author provides a good introduction to the origin and purpose of folktales in the slave communities. The collection ends with the title story, "The People Could Fly."

The Watsons Go to Birmingham—1963. Curtis, Christopher Paul. 1995. New York: Delacorte.

The story of the Watson family, who live in Flint, Michigan, is told by nine-year-old Kenny, who adores his five-year-old sister Joette but is constantly bullied by his thirteen-year-old brother Byron. Kenny relishes it whenever Byron gets into trouble, especially when he sets fire to toy parachuters in the bathroom. The parents finally decide to have Byron spend the summer in Birmingham with his grandmother, Mrs. Sands, who is a stern disciplinarian, hoping that she will be able to straighten Byron out. The whole family drives Byron to Birmingham. Not long after they arrive, Byron transforms into a sweet teenager, and Kenny starts to act out!

Zeely. Hamilton, Virginia. 1986. New York: Aladdin.

In this story, twelve-year-old Elizabeth "Geeder" Perry (who calls horses by shouting "Gee!") and her younger brother, John "Toeboy" Perry (who is always barefoot), spend the summer on their Uncle Ross' farm. The neighbors, Nat Tayber and his grown daughter Zeely, rent the west end of Uncle Ross' property to keep their prize razorback hogs. Zeely is a six-foot-tall young woman with high cheekbones, who always looks straight ahead and is hard to get to know. One day, Geeder finds a magazine with a picture in it of a Watutsi woman who looks just like Zeely and comes to believe that Zeely must be a Watutsi queen. Eventually, Geeder gets Zeely to warm up to her when Geeder calls her attention to a mother hog who has been hurt and is being trampled by other hogs. As the two become friends, Zeely shares with Geeder that she *is* Watutsi. Then she tells Geeder a story about the beginning of the world and a girl who waits for a message to tell her who she is and what she will do in the world. At first, Geeder is puzzled by the story. Then she realizes that it is about herself.

High School—Adult

Alice Walker. [videocassette]. Alice Walker. 1997. Princeton, NJ: Films for the Humanities and Sciences.

In this thirty-three-minute video recording Alice Walker talks about her childhood in rural Georgia, her transformation because of the Civil Rights movement, and racism and sexism.

Beloved and *Jazz*. [videocassette]. Morrison, Toni. 1997. Princeton, NJ: Films for the Humanities and Sciences.

In this twenty-nine-minute video recording Toni reads from two of her works, *Beloved* and *Jazz*, to show how she returns to the pain of slavery and segregation to restore wholeness to the African American psyche.

Black Boy (American Hunger). Wright, Richard. 1992. New York: Harper & Row.

This is the author's autobiography. Wright was born on Rucker's Plantation near Roxie, Mississippi in 1908. His four grandparents were born into slavery. His father was an illiterate sharecropper and his mother a schoolteacher. In 1913, when Richard was five years old, the father deserted the family and the mother became the sole supporter of the family by working as a cook. As soon as he is able, Wright works after school to help the family survive financially. His childhood and adolescence is described as constantly hungry and undernourished. In 1924 Wright is valedictorian, but he refuses to give the speech the principal has prepared for him, a testimony to his character that is unable to accept the second-rate citizenship. To escape the oppression of the South, Wright leaves Memphis and moves to Chicago. In 1940 Wright's novel *Native Son* receives critical acclaim as does his memoir *Black Boy* in 1945.

Go Tell It on the Mountain. Baldwin, James. [1952] 1981. New York: Dell.

This is the story of a young man, Johnny Grimes, growing up in Harlem in a poor family, whose members are mainstays of a tiny local Pentecostal church. Those who know him expect that one day he will become a great pastor, yet in his teens he begins to think of escape. This is partly because of the attractions of the world but also partly because of the hatred his abusive father Joshua, a church deacon, inspires in him. The novel concentrates on the climactic night in John's spiritual life, a night at the church where he must make the decision whether to accept Jesus as Lord or reject him forever. His parents and his aunt are there with other church members, and the book basically tells us the thoughts of each as they pray in order to give us insight into the events that shaped the Grimes family.

Jazz. Morrison, Toni. 1992. New York: Knopf.

This is the story of a childless married couple, Violet and Joe Trace, living in New York City's Harlem. Fifty-six-year-old Violet has become depressed and spends less time with her husband Joe. While selling cosmetics, Joe meets Dorcas, an eighteen-year-old girl, who lives with her aunt, Alice Manfred, because her parents were murdered in the East St. Louis riots. Joe and Dorcas have an affair; after three months Joe kills Dorcas because she has lost interest in the relationship. Violet decides to find out more about Dorcas and visits Alice, Dorca's aunt. During their visits, Alice and Violet discover they have much in common. Through this ordeal, Violet and Joe become closer. Morrison traces the violence of blacks toward other blacks back to Violet's and Joe's generations of enslavement, the violence of slavery, and the disuniting of families. (Mature subject matter)

Narrative of the Life of Frederick Douglass: An American Slave. Douglass, Frederick. [1845] 1999. New York: Oxford University Press.

This is the author's autobiography; he was born into slavery in Tuckahoe, Maryland in approximately 1818. As a house slave living in Baltimore, at the age of twelve he is taught to read and write by one of his slave mistresses, Mrs. Auld, and then at great risk to himself advances his own reading and writing when the mistress is forbidden to proceed. After reading about Catholic emancipation, Douglass decides that eventually he will free himself. At the age of sixteen Douglass becomes a field slave on a wheat plantation and bears the whippings and hard physical labor of working from sun-up to sundown. In 1938 he frees himself, marries Anna, and eventually, after working for three years, begins his public speaking career in the antislavery movement.

Vintage Hughes. Hughes, Langston. 2004. New York: Vintage.

This book includes poems from the book *Collected Poems of Langston Hughes* and three short stories from his book *The Ways of White Folks.* Langston Hughes was Zora Neale Hurston's contemporary, both writers of the Harlem Renaissance period. The poems include: "The Negro Speaks of Rivers," "Let America Be America, Again," "Georgia Dusk," "Birmingham Sunday," "The Heart of Harlem," and "Harlem [2]." Langston Hughes was awarded the Guggenheim Fellowship (1935) and membership in the American Academy of Arts and Letters (1947).

THE GENDER EXPERIENCE

Gender parity has come a long way for American women in the last hundred years. In 1920, women gained the right to vote in the United States—

allowing them to publicly participate in male-dominated politics. In the 1960s, gender parity began to include women's rights to play sports on school teams and to work in nontraditional jobs. Also, gender-neutral language entered the English language, so that, for example, *postman* was replaced by *postal worker*, *fireman* was replaced by *firefighter*, and *policeman* was replaced by *police officer*. Carol Gilligan's research on adolescent girls' (1982) and women's development has expanded the field of psychology that had previously been dominated by men. Moreover, feminist thought as a way to discuss legitimate forms of knowledge has permeated research and areas of study such as modern thought.

Gender Themes: Picture Books

Arturo y Clementina. Turin, Adela, and Nella Bosnia. 1976. Barcelona: Editorial Lumen.

This book is written in Spanish. In order to use it, we recommend that the teacher find someone who can translate it for monolingual students or non–Spanish English bilinguals. In the story, two turtles, Arturo and Clementina, fall in love. During their lives together, Clementina wants to develop her sense of self by learning to paint. Arturo tells her that she is stupid and cannot paint, but wanting to please her, he buys her a painting. In the end, Clementina leaves Arturo without telling him.

Tea with Milk. Say, Allen. 1999. Boston: Houghton Mifflin.

When May Morawaki graduates from high school in San Francisco, her parents take her back to Japan to find her a husband. Her dream, however, is to go to college and then live in San Francisco. Once in Japan, May, who is now called Masako, attends high school, where she learns to read and write Japanese. At home, she takes lessons in calligraphy, flower arranging, and traditional tea ceremonies. After her parents hire a matchmaker, she is soon matched with a young banker's son. Determined not to marry, however, she takes a bus to Osaka, lands a job as an elevator girl, and later as a store guide for foreign businessmen. Eventually, she meets a young Japanese man named Joseph, who also speaks English because his foster parents sent him to an English school. They eventually marry and move to Yokohama, where they have their first child, the author of this book. (Japanese American Literature)

Gender Themes: Young Adult Books

Her Stories. Hamilton, Virginia. 1995. New York: Blue Sky Press.

This is a collection of nineteen folktales about African American girls and women. The stories are grouped under five themes: (1) animal tales; (2) fairy tales; (3) supernatural tales; (4) folkways and legends; and (5) true stories. Each story is illustrated by one beautiful painting. The stories include the little girl who out-smarts Buh Rabbi in a trickster tale; clever Ella who, in a Cinderella-type tale, does not marry the woodsman like her father wishes but instead marries the king; the clever Malindy, who outsmarts the devil when he is ready to take her soul; and the story of when Man and Woman were equal.

USING THE GROWING UP ETHNIC:
THE AFRICAN AMERICAN EXPERIENCE THEME-SET

We recommend using the picture books and young adult books to set the stage for reading the core literature, *Their Eyes Were Watching God*. Sherley Anne Williams' foreword lays the background for the issues encountered in *Their Eyes Were Watching God*. For example, folk culture is used in literature in or-der to create a distinctive African American literary aesthetic and to eliminate the degrading stereotypes of the time (the comical Negro, exotic, little black Sambo, and so on). Williams points to the lack of available books written by African American authors before and during the Harlem Renaissance as an example of what American society was like before the 1970s.

Among other things, *Their Eyes Were Watching God* depicts the treatment of black and biracial women and the oral storytelling traditions of African Americans in 1930s America. Nevertheless, even contemporary black critics, including the novelist Richard Wright, did not think highly of the work when it came out in 1937. It was not until after the author's death in 1960 and the triumphs of the Civil Rights movement in that decade, that the book began to receive national acclaim.

In order for students to understand the novel *Their Eyes Were Watching God*, it is important to present a historical review of the African American experience. The novel spans the time period when Janie's grandmother was a slave and when she and all the slaves in the Confederate states were emancipated in 1863. *The African American Family Album* by Dorothy and Thomas Hoobler can serve as a background resource, first for the teacher and then for the students as they be-gin this theme-set. *The African American Family Album* begins with a view of life in Africa, then moves through a middle passage when Africans are transported to the New World (1442–1863), slavery and emancipation (1863), a new life in the South during reconstruction (1865–1909), the great migration from south-ern states to northern ones (1920–1950), and the Civil Rights movement (1950s–1970s). *From Slave Ship to Freedom Road* by Julius Lester depicts the live of slaves from its inception to their freedom in 1865. *Middle Passage* by Feelings specifi-cally depicts the hardships Africans had on the journey from African to the New World on the slave trade ships.

Patricia McKissack's picture book *Zora Neale Hurston, Writer and Storyteller* is a biography that would succinctly help students to learn more about the writer's life.

Although *Their Eyes Were Watching God* is set in the 1930s, a number of picture books depict the lives of African Americans in more recent times. In *Aunt Flossie's Hats*, beautiful oil paintings portray a day when Aunt Flossie's granddaughters come to visit, and Aunt Flossie reminisces about her childhood and young adult life. It parallels Janie's telling Phoebe her story of life with Nanny, Logan Killicks, Joe Starks, and Tea Cake. *Zeely*, *The Watsons Go to Birmingham—1963*, and *Black Boy* all present stories of older children and young adults growing up. In *Zeely*, Elizabeth "Geeder" Perry narrates her summer on her Uncle Ross' farm and meeting Zeely Tayber, a beautiful, extraordinarily tall young woman who looked like the tall Watutsi women of Africa. Geeder grows from her meeting and talking with Zeely. In *The Watsons Go to Birmingham—1963*, Kenny, a nine-year-old, narrates his story of growing up with an older brother and the trip they took to Birmingham, Mississippi to spend the summer with Grandma Sands. Lastly, in *Black Boy*, Richard Wright, a contemporary of Zora Neale Hurston, writes his memoir about growing up in the South. The autobiography moves from childhood to adulthood.

Tar Beach and *Aunt Harriet's Underground Railroad* use the metaphor of flying to escape to freedom. *Tar Beach* is about a young girl who imagines herself to be free to fly. Janie returns to Eatonville, Florida to her home where she and Joe lived as a couple. Janie sees herself as free to think about Tea Cake and to relish her life. She is childless and so does not have the responsibility of mothering a child.

The African American experience can be further explored by reading *A Place Called Freedom*, which presents an all-black town similar to Eatonville, Florida where Joe and Janie Starks move and help build in *Their Eyes*. The townspeople of Eatonville sit on Joe Stark's porch and tell stories. Virginia Hamilton's *The People Could Fly* is a compilation of folktales that slaves told each other to enable them to endure their fate and give themselves hope. Moreover, Hamilton's *Her Stories*, too, are folktales but feature female protagonists. Mildred Taylor's *Roll of Thunder, Gold Cadillac*, and *The Friendship* are stories that illustrate the lives of African Americans during the Jim Crow laws. Christopher Paul Curtis' *The Watsons Go to Birmingham—1963* and Dr. Martin Luther King's speech (1999) are set during the Civil Rights movement.

Conceptions of Beauty

Conceptions of beauty are sprinkled throughout the novel. Janie is considered a beautiful woman by her three husbands. Logan Killicks refers to her as a "LilBit"; Joe Starks refers to her as a "pretty doll-baby" (49). Moreover, Joe wants her to look at herself as a "bell cow" and the other women as "her followers" (66). Questions that can be discussed include: What is beauty? How is physical beauty portrayed in the novel? How is physical beauty portrayed today in mainstream magazines and in magazines specifically for African American women? in movies? in commercials? How does age affect our conceptions of beauty in girls and women in comparison with boys and men? How is beauty different among different ethnic, racial, and social groups? How does the media perceive ethnic beauty? In 1983 Vanessa Williams was crowned Miss

America, the first African American woman to win the title. How many African American women have subsequently won the Miss America title?

Zora Neale Hurston makes several references to long heavy hair that falls down Janie's back, a symbol of beauty in the book. Joe Starks sees and admires Janie's hair as she is pumping the water (47). Janie's grandmother, when she was young, had long beautiful hair; the author tells us that Mr. Roberts, the plantation owner, before he left to fight the North, "wropped his hand around her hair" (33); Walter touches the loose end of Janie's braided hair in the store, unbeknownst to Janie, but Joe sees the scene. He is outraged and instructs his wife to cover her hair with a head rag from then on, believing he is the only man who should view this intimate and very beautiful feature. What constitutes beautiful hair? Janie's biraciality has given her long, smooth hair. Where does the curly hair of African Americans fit into the conception of beauty? What hairstyles are common among African American women now and in the past?

Ethnic and Racial Identity

Janie's background is biracial back to her grandmother's generation. Nanny had a baby (Janie's mother) by the white slave master, Mr. Roberts, and Janie's father, the schoolteacher was also white. However, neither her grandmother nor Janie seems to relate to their white European ancestry but rather identify themselves as black. During the writing of the novel (in the 1930s) how did society view biraciality? How does society view biraciality today? How did the U.S. Census take into account biraciality? How does Neale Hurston present the power differentials in a slave–master relationship?

Joe Starks chooses an all-black community in which to live. What drives him to seek such a community? There are two additional points in the novel, at the beginning and at the end, where racial identity comes to the forefront. Nanny's story as a young woman is tied to the white family who owned the plantation on which she worked as a slave. After the Emancipation Proclamation, Nanny leaves with a white woman, Mrs. Washburn, who Nanny feels will provide protection for her and her daughter, and in turn, Nanny will help care for Mrs. Washburn's grandchildren. Two paintings from Lester's book, *From Slave Ship to Freedom Road*, portray this life-changing event for both blacks and whites: in the painting titled *Then Came the Word*, the Union soldier on his horse and the slave owner inform the slaves in the fields that they should stop working because they are free. In the painting *Goodbye Mississippi Autumn*, a group of men, women, and children leave the plantation, and the author writes that although many left to search for their wives and children, many slaves also stayed. They did not know what freedom meant after generations of living in slavery. In *Their Eyes Were Watching God*, Nanny leaves to make a life of her own with her daughter. Nanny leaves, however, with Mrs. Washburn, a white woman, to help care for her children—a similar but not identical role to that which Nanny served on the plantation when she was a slave. Julius Lester in *From Slave Ship to Freedom Road* ends the book with this same issue of how freedom is conceptualized after years of oppression and controlling laws.

Gender Roles in Relationships

Marriage and divorce are major life-changing events. American conceptions of marriage and family have changed from the 1900–1950s to the 1960s and again to the present day. Zora Neale Hurston portrays Janie as passive, subordinated, and proactive in her relationships with her three husbands: Logan Killicks, Joe Starks, and Vergible Tea Cake Woods.

One gender phenomenon exhibited in many traditions and attitudes worldwide is the subordination of women in marriage relationships. It is the power of one individual over another, and it results in the daily verbal and nonverbal indignities to which an individual with less power is subjected. It is an issue that has been widely discussed, and because of it, the roles of men and women in marriage have changed. As women work outside the home, men are taking more responsibility in the domestic chores. In Janie and Joe's relationship, Janie is first subordinated by Joe at the dedication ceremony of the lampposts that will light the streets in the new town. The crowd asks that Janie say a few words, but Joe immediately interrupts the applause and answers for Janie, "Thank you fuh yo' compliments, but mah wife don't know nothin' 'bout no speech-makin.' Ah never married her for nothin' lak dat. She's uh woman and her place is in de home" (69). Although Janie had not thought about giving a speech, she believes that it is the way Joe speaks out without consulting with her or giving her the opportunity to respond that is demeaning. Why? What drives her to stay in the marriage even though she has come to compromise her values and dreams? Compare the Janie-Joe incident at the dedication of the lamps with scenes from the picture book, *Arturo y Clementina*, in which Arturo is portrayed as a domineering husband. The wife, Clementina, shares her desires to learn to play the flute and to paint with her husband, Arturo. At first, he opposes her wishes. But then, thinking better of it, he patronizes her by buying her a phonograph to listen to flute music and a painting so that she may admire good art. Clementina leaves him in the end without warning. How are women subordinated in marriage relationships? How are men subordinated in marriage relationships? How are people in other types of relationship subordinated? How is that subordination justified?

In a second comparison, Janie holds her own with Logan as he tries to get her to work outside, helping him with the farm work, but Janie, too, leaves her first husband without saying anything. In contrast, Tea Cake, her third husband, asks her to move to Jacksonville, Florida to work alongside him, cutting sugar cane and cooking for the after-work parties. She seems to do all of these things willingly. Does Tea Cake feel subordinated in his relationship? Does Janie feel subordinated in their relationship? Does money play a part in subordination? When Janie marries Tea Cake, she has a big house and money in the bank. Does this financial situation liberate her to engage as an equal in the relationship with Tea Cake?

In *Their Eyes Were Watching God* there are two types of stories: (1) autobiographical stories people tell about themselves, and (2) stories that entertain or have a message to convey. In the beginning of the novel, Janie tells Phoebe the story about her own development from a young teenage girl to a mature woman. Telling our own story to people to whom we are close is a common human experience. How does telling our story help us actualize ourselves and make sense of events in our lives? Compare Janie's telling of her own story to Phoebe with the stories Aunt Flossie tells her grandnieces in *Aunt Flossie's Hats*.

The second type of stories is told by Sam and Liggee on the store porch. The mule story is the one that is the most prominent in the novel *Their Eyes*. What purpose do these stories serve? Why does Janie relish these stories, and why does Joe not want her hearing those stories? The stories told in the core novel can be compared and contrasted with stories from the picture books and young adult books such as Virginia Hamilton's *Her Stories* and Robert San Souci's *The Faithful Friend* and *The Talking Eggs*. Some of these stories were intended merely to entertain while others were meant to help slaves cope with the aggression and violence they experienced on the plantations. Virginia Hamilton's quintessential book, *The People Could Fly*, uses the metaphor "flying to freedom" as a mechanism for coping with the psychologically damaging horrors of slavery. Faith Ringgold in *Tar Beach* also uses this metaphor in a contemporary setting.

Language

In the novel *Their Eyes Were Watching God*, Zora Neale Hurston uses both Standard English (SE) and African American Vernacular English (AAVE), using SE in the narrative portion and AAVE in the dialogue to authentically portray her characters. A short linguistic study of AAVE will allow students to understand how AAVE combined African grammatical structures with English.

Researchers argue that AAVE originated as a pidgin, a *lingua franca,* that was created by speakers of different languages who were in constant contact and needed to communicate with one another in the slave trade and on plantations (Rickford 1992; Smitherman 1977, 1994; Todd 1990). A pidgin "is no one's native language" (Rickford 1992, 224). In its inception as a pidgin, AAVE evolved from combining the grammar and sounds of several African languages and English vocabulary in order for the slaves to communicate among one another and with the slave owners (Rickford 1992, 242). As the children of the pidgin-speaking parents used the pidgin for varied reasons and as they had more contact with English speakers, the pidgin evolved into a more sophisticated language known as a *creole*, similar to Hawaiian Creole English or Jamaican Creole English.

Several of the children's books and young adult books, as well as the core literature selection, contain the linguistic variety of the African American people across gender, age, class, and geographical regions. For example, Zora Neale Hurston's *Their Eyes Were Watching God* uses southern black vernacular with corresponding spelling (for example, *dere* for *there*). Virginia Hamilton, too, in one of her folktales set in the Sea Islands off South Carolina uses the Gullah language (for example, *dayclean* for *dawn*). In Christopher Paul Curtis' *The Watsons Go to Birmingham—1963*, some characters such as the grandmother, who lives in Mississippi, use the vernacular. But the Watson family living in Flint, Michigan uses SE. Many of the other novels use both, the vernacular in conversations but the standard in the narration. How is the vernacular used in *Their Eyes*? Toni Morrison, in the *New Republic*, commented about the use of the vernacular in her novels: "The worst of all possible things that could happen would be to lose that language. There are certain things I cannot say without recourse to my language. . . . I know the standard. I want to use it to help restore the lingua franca" (LeClair 1981, 27).

In Figure 4–1, we provide a summary of the discourse, syntactical, lexical, and phonological features if teachers would like to use it with their students (Labov 1970, 113; Rickford 1992; Smitherman 1994). In this linguistic study students should note that all language variations, including AAVE, are rule-governed, that is, there are specific rules that govern any language or dialect—communication is not a free-for-all or "anything goes."

In the novel *Their Eyes Were Watching God*, the spectators mention that Joe and Janie are "playing the dozens," which is a recognized discourse feature. "Playing the dozens" is "a verbal ritual of talking negatively about someone's mother, (occasionally grandmothers and other female relatives) by coming up with outlandish, highly exaggerated, often sexually loaded, humorous 'insults'" (Smitherman 1994, 99). Other discourse features include exaggeration and call and response.

Discourse features. Discourse is a genre or form of language that serves a particular communicative function, such as a joke, personal letter, or expository essay.

Syntactical features. West African languages allow for the construction of the following types of sentences or syntactical features. The empty sign "Ø" represents the absent place in which a word would be used in SE.

1. the absence of *is* and *are* in present tense states and actions, such as "Where Ø yo' husband at?" (*Their Eyes Were Watching God* 1978, 49)
2. the absence of the third person tense *-s*: "He lookØ like some ole skull head in de grave yard." (28)

Lexical features. AAVE uses words of West African language origins such as *yam* (sweet potato) from the Wolof word *nyam*. Other West African language words include *tater, turnip, banana,* and *banjo* (Rickford 1992, 295). In the novel, both Janie and Logan used the word *tators* for *potatoes* and the word *tote*. The following are examples of the West African origin lexicon in the following phrases:

1. ". . . you oughta be able tuh tote it inside." (45)
2. ". . . cut up dese seed tators fuh me." (46)

African Origin Discourse Style

1. playing the dozens: "a verbal ritual of talking negatively about someone's mother, (occasionally grandmothers and other female relatives) by coming up with outlandish, highly exaggerated, often sexually loaded, humorous 'insults'" (Smitherman 1994, 99)

Examples

See *Their Eyes*, pages 121–123 (Joe and Janie)

2. exaggeration: the mule stories in *Their Eyes*

See page 87 (Sam and Lige)

3. call and response: a constant back-and-forth response between two individuals or a preacher and the congregants in church sermons

See page 97 (Joe Starks at the mule ceremony)

African Origin Syntactical Features

1. the absence of *is* and *are* in present-tense states and actions

2. the use of the invariant *be* to express habitual aspect

Examples

"Where ∅ yo' husband at?" (49)

"Sometime I still be sleeping" or "It be cold, cold, cold" [habitually cold] for the standard English. "Sometimes I am still sleeping" or "It is cold, cold, cold" (Williams 1992, 1, 3)

3. the absence of the third-person tense *-s*

"He look∅ like some ole skull head in de grave yard." (28)

African Origin Lexical Features

Wolof language
other West African language

Examples

yam (sweet potato) from the Wolof word *nyam*

tater, turnip, banana, and *banjo*

African Influence Phonological Features

reduction of two consonants to one at the end of a word

1. the deletion of /d/ and /t/

Examples

tol [told], and *chile* [child]

an' [and], *jus'*, [just]

FIGURE 4–1 *Summary of Linguistic Features of African American Vernacular English*

Phonological features. Common phonological features found in the dialogue of *Their Eyes* include the following:

1. Initial /th/ = /d/
   Examples: them = dem; then = den; the = de; that = dat
2. Final /th/ = /f/
   Examples: mouth = mouf; tooth = toof; south = souf; first = fust; with = wid
3. Medial and final /r/ = deleted (similar to a Bostonian deletion of the /r/)
   Examples: for = fuh; yourself = yo'self; more = mo'; lord = lawd
4. Final two consonants are reduced to one consonant, especially when /t/ or /d/ is the second member
   Examples: chi<u>ld</u> = chile; to<u>ld</u> = tol'; a<u>nd</u> = an'; ju<u>st</u> = jus

ACTIVITIES USING MULTIPLE INTELLIGENCES

Each activity that incorporates one or more of Gardner's eight intelligences has been designed to be completed while the students follow Janie from one location or "milestone" to another.

Milestone 1: Janie's Life with Her Grandmother (Chapters 1–2)

On a late afternoon Nanny had called her to come inside the house because she had spied Janie letting Johnny Taylor kiss her over the gatepost. (23)

1. The students write out and then respond to Zora Neale Hurston's first paragraph:

   Ships at a distance have every man's wish on board. For some they come in with the tide. For some they sail forever on the horizon, never out of sight, never landing until the Watcher turns his eye in resignation, his dreams mocked away by time. That is the life of men. (9)

   This quote can be juxtaposed with Lomas Garza's painting *Beds for Dreaming* in her book *Family Pictures/Cuadros de familia* (1990). The students should look at the details of the pictures, asking numerous questions. For example, Where are the girls? What are they pointing to? What could they be discussing? Where is the mother, and what might she be thinking as she makes the bed? The students can then read Lomas Garza's paragraph in which she states her own ideas about the painting *Beds for Dreaming*. Another form of dreaming is the vision Dr. Martin Luther King Jr. had for humanity in his famous speech, "I Have a Dream." The students should read that speech and outline what King's dream entailed. (Visual, Linguistic)
2. The students create a chronology of Nanny's and Janie's lives using two separate timelines. Students will have to use approximate dates based on events in the novel. A third timeline can be drawn to

include the historical context of their lives. (Spatial and Logical-Mathematical)

For example, students should include the following dates and events:

a. British order that black servants would be held in perpetual slavery (1664).
b. Quakers publish pamphlets condemning slavery (1688).
c. Northern states abolish slavery: Vermont (1777); New Jersey (1804); New York (1827).
d. Civil War (1861) begins.
e. Thirteenth Amendment abolishes slavery in the United States (1865).
f. Southern Homestead Act (1866) opens government-owned lands in five states to African American settlers.
g. Fourteenth Amendment guarantees former slaves citizens full constitutional rights (1868).
h. U.S. Supreme Court rules in *Plessey v. Ferguson* that "separate but equal" facilities are constitutional enabling states to pass Jim Crow Laws (1896).
i. National Association for the Advancement of Colored People (NAACP) is founded (1909).
j. Civil Rights Law signed (1964).
k. Voting Rights Act (1965) passed.

Nanny's Life

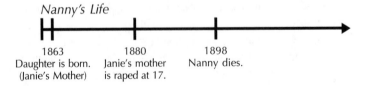

1863	1880	1898
Daughter is born. (Janie's Mother)	Janie's mother is raped at 17.	Nanny dies.

Historical Context

1863
Emancipation
Proclamation

Janie's Life

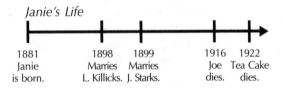

1881	1898	1899	1916	1922
Janie is born.	Marries L. Killicks.	Marries J. Starks.	Joe dies.	Tea Cake dies.

3. The students read George Ella Lyon's poem "Where I'm From" several times, once to themselves and twice with a partner (partner A reads it aloud while B listens; then partner B reads it aloud while A listens). The teacher and students discuss and respond to the poem.

    a. Each student writes his or her own version of "Where I'm From," and then the students share their newly created poems with each other. The poems can be typed and bound into a book of class poems. (Christiansen 2002, 20) (Linguistic, Interpersonal)

    b. The students begin writing a "Where I'm From" poem for Janie. As they read the novel, they add more to the poem. They can revise the poem, especially as they finish the book and have new insights. This is an ongoing activity. (Linguistic, Interpersonal)

    c. For homework, the students can add a "Where I'm From" collage to their poems by using personal photographs, magazine pictures, or computer graphics. (Spatial)

4. The students create a map of Florida that fits an 8.5-by- 11-inch sheet of paper. Then each student highlights the towns and cities that mark Janie's milestones. This, too, is an ongoing activity. The map can be embellished with details. (Spatial)

Milestone 2: Janie's Married Life with Logan Killicks at His Sixty-Acre Farm (Chapters 3–4)

Janie and Logan married in Nanny's parlor on a Saturday evening with three cakes and big platters of fried rabbit and chicken. (39)

1. The students interview a minister, mullah, priest, rabbi, justice of the peace, married couple, or one or both of their parents to discuss the moral and legal requirements that a couple should consider before marriage, and then they write a report about the interview. Alternatively, the students can research the vows that couples take, including those scripted by various religious groups and those that couples create themselves. (Linguistic, Intrapersonal, Interpersonal)

2. Students are assigned to read about prearranged marriages and romantic marriages and to compare and contrast the two types in a short essay. This assignment can be done in pairs, with partner A researching one type of marriage and partner B researching the other. The members of each pair meet to share information and create a compare-and-contrast chart from which they can then write separate essays or one joint essay. The students report back to the class as a whole on "What is an ideal marriage?" (Linguistic, Interpersonal, Spatial)

3. Students are asked whether parents and relatives discuss the issue of who their children should marry. They write their thoughts in a journal. (Linguistic, Intrapersonal, Interpersonal)

4. Students conduct a brief linguistic study by investigating different aspects of language use, which includes the larger sections of text and oral language, such as a conversation or a story told on Joe Starks' porch

(discourse); individual sentences (syntactical); vocabulary (lexical); and sounds in words (phonological). For this linguistic study, the students may use the core text only, or they may include other books as well. The picture book *Working Cotton* by Sherley Anne Williams uses both the Standard English and vernacular and can be used as part of the linguistic study. Figure 4–1 provides a reference for students to use as a guide for this linguistic study. Divide the students into linguistic study groups: group 1 looks at examples of discourse features; group 2, syntactical or sentence features; group 3, lexical or vocabulary or individual words; group 4, phonological or sound features within words. (Linguistic)

Milestone 3: Janie's Married Life with Joe Starks in the Utopian Town, Eatonville, Florida (Chapters 5–9)

"Green Cove Springs," he told the driver. So they were married there before sundown, just like Joe had said. With new clothes of silk and wool. (55)

1. To see what it was like for Joe to open his grocery store, the students should research what it takes to start a small business. If there are licenses involved, what are the fees? Are there other requirements, such as posting the business' fictitious name in the local newspaper? The students may interview a city employee involved with such matters and report back both orally and in writing, citing their sources. (Linguistic, Intrapersonal, Interpersonal)

2. To see what it was like for Joe to become the mayor of Eatonville, a group of students may interview the mayor and city council members of their own city or town. Alternatively, the mayor and city council members may be invited to class as guest speakers or may be interviewed in class by the assigned group. In order for the interviews to be productive for the mayor and city council members, the students need to be prepared with questions ahead of time. They should be instructed to brainstorm questions and then turn these in to be proofed by the teacher, after which the questions should be typed in their final format. The students may also mail their questions to the mayor and city council members as part of a letter. (Linguistic, Intrapersonal, Interpersonal)

3. A second group of students may attend a city council meeting, where they take notes on the discussion pros and cons and indicate which items pass, fail, or are tabled for later discussion. The students may follow up by obtaining the minutes of the meeting and then making oral reports to the class. (Interpersonal, Linguistic)

4. To appreciate Hurston's use of folklore in the novel, the students should select and read one of the seventy folktales in the first section of her book *Mules and Men* ([1935] 1990). The folktales are presented one after another. The students should use the table of contents, which has

the titles of the tales, to locate specific ones in the text. The teacher should note that the second part of the book is Zora Neale Hurston's collection of Hoodoo rituals from her ethnographic study in Jamaica. The students may also collect folktales from home and share them with the class. (Linguistic, Interpersonal) Another twist on this assignment is to have students research folk songs, gospel songs, jazz, or ballads from the late 1930s and share one or two they really like, focusing on the story in the song. (Musical)

5. A critical turning point in the novel and in Joe and Janie's relationship comes when they play the dozens publicly. "'Great God of Zion!' Sam Watson gasped. 'Y'all really playin' the dozens tuhnight'" (123). Reread pages 121–123 to analyze how Janie plays the dozens with Joe Starks and what the community witnesses. How does Janie and Joe's relationship change because their conversation is public and neither is able to "save face"? Definitions and historical explanations of playing the dozens can be found under the heading "Language," p. 50. Also see Geneva Smitherman's *Black Talk: Words and Phrases from the Hood to the Amen Corner* (1994). What causes Janie to be put in this position? What causes Joe to be put in this position as well? How does their relationship change after this? What could have prevented the relationship from alienating both of them? What could be done to improve their relationship? (Linguistic, Intrapersonal, Interpersonal)

Milestone 4: Janie's Courtship and Married Life with Tea Cake in Jacksonville, Florida, and in the Everglades (Chapters 10–20)

And there was Tea Cake in the big old station in a new blue suit and straw hat, hauling her off to a preacher's house first thing. (173)

1. Students research information about the following topics that come up in the novel:
   a. the Everglades
   b. rabies
   c. hurricanes
   e. floods
   d. loss of a loved one
   e. widows and widowers
   f. folklore stories
   g. AAVE and regional variations

   The students report back orally in class and in a written report. (Linguistic)

2. In the core text Janie sees several bands of Seminole Indians leaving the Everglades for the east where there is high ground. What signs does nature give telling them that a hurricane and flood are about to happen? Later in the day, Janie sees hordes of snakes and possums also heading east, and at night the larger animals such as the deer and panthers

follow them. Do animals sense the hurricane coming in their feet, in the temperature in the air, or in other ways? Research how animals know that a natural disaster is looming, and include this in a report. (Linguistic, Naturalist)

Milestone 5: Janie Returns to Her House in Eatonville, Florida (Chapter 20)

They had begged Janie to stay on with them and she had stayed a few weeks to keep them from feeling bad. . . . She had given away everything in their little house except a package of garden seeds that Tea Cake had bought to plant. . . . Now that she was home, she meant to plant them for remembrance. (238)

1. In an essay, the students describe Janie and how she has matured from the time she was seventeen and living with her grandmother. How have her dreams changed?
2. Students write out the quote below and then respond to it in their journals.

   She pulled in her horizon like a great fish-net. Pulled it from around the waist of the world and draped it over her shoulder. So much life in its meshes. She called in her soul to come see. (236).

3. Students should compare and contrast the quote above with the opening paragraph of the book.

   Ships at a distance have every man's wish on board. For some they come in with the tide. For some they sail forever on the horizon, never out of sight, never landing until the Watcher turns his eye in resignation, his dreams mocked away by time. That is the life of men. (9)

   What does the fish-net quote tell us about Janie as an older woman? Why does the author end the book this way?

4. Students complete their "Where I'm From" poem for Janie.

Culmination: Milestones 1–5

1. Adding recorded instrumental music of their own choice, the students read their completed "Where I'm From" poems for Janie to the class. (Musical)
2. For all the towns and cities highlighted on their Florida maps, students do some background research about what these places are like today and discuss their findings in class. (Spatial, Linguistic, Interpersonal)
3. In literacy circles of four to six, students develop collaborative posters on one of Janie's five milestones. Each poster should contain two quotes that present critical details from the story, one original phrase that depicts the central idea of the story and a symbol that describes one of the following: (1) Janie's life; (2) the life of a secondary character; or (3) a setting in the story. (Linguistic, Interpersonal, Bodily-Kinesthetic)

4. When the students finish reading the novel, their collaborative posters should be displayed in the classroom, and all the students should participate in a gallery walk, the way people do in museums or art galleries. To make this process more engaging, each literacy circle will select two of its members to serve as docents, who will stay with the group's poster and explain it to the others. For the first half of the gallery walk, one docent from each group will remain at the group's poster, and then the other one will take over, so that each one will have a chance to participate in the walk. (Linguistic, Interpersonal, Bodily-Kinesthetic)

Zora Neale Hurston Chronology

1901: Zora Neale Hurston is born in Alabama but claims Eatonville, Florida as her birthplace.

1920s: Harlem in New York City is where many "New Negroes" arrive to establish the artistic capital of black America.

1925: Hurston begins a two-year study with Franz Boas at Columbia University in cultural anthropology. Ruth Benedict is Boas' assistant.

1928: Hurston receives her B.A. from Barnard College.

1928: Hurston begins her collection of folklore in the South through Mrs. Osgood Mason, who financed a two-year study in Florida, Alabama, Louisiana, and the West Indies.

1932: Hurston organized and funded a show, *The Great Day*, at the John Golden Theater that dramatized events of a day in a railroad camp [January 10 in New York].

1933: Hurston produced three folk concerts.

1934: *Jonas Gourd Vine* is published.

1935: *Mules and Men* is published.

1936: Hurston received a Guggenheim fellowship to study magic practices in the West Indies.

1937: *Their Eyes Are Watching God* is published.

1938: *Tell My Horse* is published.

1939: *Moses, Man of the Mountain* is published.

1942: *Dust Tracks on a Road: An Autobiography* is published.

1948: *Seraph on the Suwanee* is published.

5 | THEME-SET 3: LITERATURE OF WAR

Core Text: Night *by Elie Wiesel*

Learning to form substantive philosophies that are supportable when challenged from any direction builds people of strong character who will take an active role in the democratic process. It is an active, informed constituency whose voices are most needed when this country is faced with the prospect of going to war. Having been secondary students during the Vietnam War, we recognize the impact that war, even one so far away, can have on the minds and emotions of teenagers. How do we balance the conflicting points of view about the necessity of armed intervention? Students already come to us with entrenched ideas about the world that are gained from, among other things, song lyrics, television, movie plots, and discussions at the dinner table. As educators, our job is to ask the hard questions repeatedly, pushing and prodding, offering the best literature and research opportunities we can find to expand our students' perspectives. One way we can do this is to provide a historical retrospective about wars fought during a variety of generations viewed through the eyes of children, men and women, and soldiers and victims. This type of interdisciplinary approach also provides avenues to understanding that history alone may not. We want our students to develop their own views based on objective and subjective accounts and to be ready to defend their views using historical, psychological, and literary evidence to explain them.

When selecting a core text for the Literature of War theme-set, we felt that it was important to choose a real-life account that has been highly acclaimed and presents the crucible of war through the eyes of a young person. Elie Wiesel's *Night* (1960), a book gaining popularity in secondary classrooms, meets all of our criteria and presents themes of rich texture that prompt the hard questions we want students to ask about war, their own identity, and their sense of humanity as a whole.

Night, a story divided into nine unnumbered segments, is the account of Elie Wiesel's grueling experiences in several concentration camps near the end of World War II. Elie is only fourteen years old when he and his family of devoutly religious Jews are forced to leave their home in Sighet, Romania in the spring of 1944. He and his fifty-year-old father are separated from his mother and three sisters when their train arrives at Auschwitz, Poland. They enter the camp through Birkenau, the reception center for the Auschwitz compound, and lie about their ages in order to stay together in the group of able-bodied men, Elie claiming to be eighteen and his father, forty. The process of dehumanization begins when vicious trustees strip them of their clothes as part of the process of selection of who will be allowed to live and toil in the camp. The barber shaves their heads; they take a shower to disinfect their bodies; they are given ill-fitting prison clothes; and they are herded into a mud-floored barracks. Before marching to a new camp, Buna, they live for three weeks with SS officers menacing them with machine guns, revolvers, and dogs.

While in Buna, Elie experiences so much inhumanity, he begins to doubt the existence of a silent God who would allow such atrocities. Particularly difficult for him is the hanging of a small, angelic-looking thirteen-year-old who weighs so little that he takes over half an hour to die of strangulation.

With the Red Army approaching Buna, the prisoners are forced to leave Buna on foot for a "safer" location. Many prisoners die on the long run through the snow to Gleiwitz where so many men are heaped into barracks that hundreds more die of suffocation. Throughout this the ordeal, Elie manages to keep track of his ailing father. They are pressed into a car of a roofless cattle train, where Wiesel must defend his father from men who would kill him for his crust of bread. When they arrive at Buchenwald late at night, out of the hundred prisoners in his car, only twelve have survived. By this time, Elie's father is suffering from dysentery, and though other prisoners encourage Elie to eat his father's crust of bread himself, Elie does all that he can to keep his father alive, even giving him the remains of his own soup. At dawn on January 29, 1945, Elie wakes and finds that another prisoner occupies his father's bunk. He realizes that he has been relieved from a terrible burden. He joins six hundred inmates on the children's block and waits in a state of suspended animation for nearly three months until the American tanks arrive at the gates. After a bout with food poisoning, Elie finally brings himself to look in the mirror and is unable to forget the death mask of a face that looks back at him.

Once again, students will read about a number of themes, concepts, and issues in the core text, *Night*, which can be developed through the accompanying children's picture and chapter books, the young adult texts, and the adult-level reading. They will experience the confusion, fear, and loss suffered by protagonists in books at all levels as well as the strength of the human spirit that allows us to go on after great personal trauma and disasters on a scale equal to humanity itself. The themes that teachers choose to pursue will shape the selection of books from the following list as, of course, will the addition of personal favorites not identified here.

LITERATURE OF WAR

Core Literature

Night. Wiesel, Elie. 1960. New York: Hill and Wang.

Wiesel's novel is fiction but is closely based on his own experiences in four concentration camps during the Holocaust. The teenage main character feels guilty for surviving the camps that killed his family. The novel explores the boy's experiences in the camps that cause him to question how God could let such a thing happen.

Picture Books

Baseball Saved Us. Mochizuki, Ken. 1995. New York: Lee and Low.

After a brief glimpse at the way his family was removed from their home and moved to a Japanese internment camp during World War II, "Shorty" tells of how the camp's inhabitants use baseball as a diversion from their untenable circumstances. Shorty, smaller than the rest of the kids, usually is ineffective at the plate, but during one game he spies a guard as he's about to bat and channels his frustration into his swing, hitting a game-winning homerun. Even after Shorty returns home, refocusing the anger he feels when subjected to racial taunts, he finds success at a sport he has come to love.

Boxes for Katje. Fleming, Candace. 2003. New York: Farrar, Straus & Giroux.

Based on the real experiences of her mother, Candace Fleming tells a heart-warming story about how one person can make a difference. The tiny Dutch town of Olst is left in ruin after World War II. The people have little food, repatched thinning clothing, and little hope. Rosie, an American girl from Mayfield, Indiana, sends a surprise box to Katje, her pen pal in Olst. Her generosity sets off a relief effort that enables the town to survive a very cold winter.

Li'l Dan, the Drummer Boy: A Civil War Story. Bearden, Romare. 1993. New York: Simon & Schuster.

This recently discovered book, written and illustrated by renowned American artist, Romare Bearden, tells the story of Li'l Dan, who learns to play a drum while a slave on the Hollis Plantation. After black Union soldiers come one day and tell him he is free, Dan has no place to go, so he follows them and becomes their mascot. When Confederate soldiers attack, he uses his drum to warn his friends and saves their lives, warranting congratulations from General Sherman himself. The story, although worthy, is secondary to the compelling mixed-media paintings whose rich colors and bold black outlines show the influence of abstract expressionism.

So Far from the Sea. Bunting, Eve. 1998. New York: Clarion.

Laura Iwasaki and her parents make one last trek to Manzanar to visit the grave of her grandfather who, along with her father and grandmother, was interned there during World War II along with 10,000 other Japanese Americans. Grandfather, a tuna fisherman, had insisted his son wear his Boy Scout uniform on the day the soldiers came so they would know he was a true American. Laura, before the family's move to Boston, makes one final offering to the grandfather whom she never knew—her father's Boy Scout necker-chief. The illustrator contrasts tense 1940s scenes depicted in black and white and serene watercolor scenes of the 1970s.

The Wall. Bunting, Eve. 1990. New York: Clarion.

A boy and his father visit the Vietnam War Memorial to look for the boy's grandfather's name. They find it, and even though they are proud of him, they would rather have him still in their lives. The book portrays a subtle message about the Vietnam War, but its true power is in what it doesn't say. The questions the boy doesn't ask become the questions of those who read the text. A great discussion starter.

Additional Picture Books

These are a more mature selection given the nature of picture books about war.

I Never Saw Another Butterfly: Children's Drawings and Poems from Terezin Concentration Camp 1942–1944. Volavkova, Hana. 1994. New York: Schocken.

This powerful perspective on war is drawn through pictures and poetry of the children who passed through Terezin Concentration Camp. Of 15,000 children under the age of fifteen who were imprisoned there, only 100 survived. The positive, supportive attitude of one compassionate woman, also a prisoner, encouraged them to express their deepest hopes, fears, and dreams as well as to come to terms with their daily misery through creative expressions that live on to remind us of how the most innocent among us are affected by the atrocities of war.

Let the Celebrations Begin. Wild, Margaret. 1991. New York: Orchard.

Twelve-year-old Miriam, while in a Nazi liberation camp, helps the older women to make stuffed toys. Using scraps of their own ragged clothes, the women make toys for the few children remain-ing in preparation for a celebration when they are liberated. Though in a very dire situation, the women are full of hope. This work of love conveys a sophisticated message about man's in-humanity to man contrasted with the will to live and to create a moment of joy for others.

Maus: A Survivor's Tale: My Father Bleeds History. Spiegelman, Art. 1986. New York: Pantheon.

After interviewing his father, Vladek, a Holocaust survivor living outside New York City, the author uses animals in graphic novel form to bear witness to his father's experiences. This first book in the two-book set begins with Vladek's happy life as a child in prewar Poland and follows his family until they go into hiding as the Final Solution is employed by Hitler.

Maus II: A Survivor's Tale: And Here My Troubles Began. Spiegelman, Art. 1992. New York: Pantheon.

The second installment of Spiegelman's biographical graphic work about his father's experiences during the Holocaust, this book details his father's survival in the concentration camp and his final reunion with his wife.

Passage to Freedom: The Sugihara Story. Mochizuki, Ken. 1997. New York: Lee and Low.

Told in first person from the point of view of Hiroki Sugihara, son of the Japanese consul in Lithuania in 1940, this book is a portrait in conscience and courage. Defying official government orders, Mr. Sugihara personally signed travel visas from dawn to dark for hundreds of Jews who crossed into Lithuania after Germans invaded their native Poland. He was only able to assist them for one month before he was reassigned to Berlin, but his act of personal heroism contributed to the survival of hundreds of men, women, and children living in desperate times.

Pink and Say. Polacco, Patricia. 1994. New York: Philomel.

Sheldon "Say" Curtis, badly wounded during the Civil War, is saved and carried home by Pinkus "Pink" Aylee, an African American Union soldier, to Pink's mother, who cares for Say. Marauders kill Pink's mother, and the boys are captured by Confederate soldiers and sent to Andersonville prison camp. Pink is hanged the first day, but Say survives to pass along the story of the boys' connection to the rest of his family (his character is based on Polacco's great-great-grandfather).

Rose Blanche. Innocenti, Roberto. 1985. St. Paul, MN: Creative Education.

Rose Blanche, a German schoolgirl during World War II, observes soldiers when they arrest a boy and then follows them to a concentration camp. Throughout the war she smuggles food to the prisoners undetected, but ironically, on the day of the town's liberation, she is shot by soldiers. Rose is the only brightly colored individual in the story, her figure set against a backdrop of drab buildings, soldiers, and townspeople. Although a simply told story with the appearance of a picture book, this text will require interpretation for many students as the details of a concentration camp are not named or explained, and the death of Rose Blanche is merely implied. Its subtlety and impact make this book more appropriate for older children and certainly for the students in a secondary classroom.

Young Adult

Across Five Aprils. Hunt, Irene. 1964. Chicago: Follett.

Jethro Creighton, a hardworking, intelligent boy grows up when his brothers and a beloved teacher leave to fight in the Civil War. Jethro comes of age as he is left with the responsibility of the family farm. The book portrays a balanced look at both sides of the war and goes beyond the concept of war itself to show the importance of family and loyalty.

Anne Frank: The Diary of a Young Girl. Frank, Anne. 1958. New York: Globe.

Anne Frank begins keeping her diary when she is thirteen, just before going into hiding from the Nazis with her family. Her diary chronicles the struggles common to adolescents—relationships with family and friends, emerging sexuality—while also chronicling her experiences in hiding during the war.

Briar Rose. Yolen, Jane. 2002. New York: Starscape.

Yolen links the Sleeping Beauty fairy tale with a story of the Holocaust. Rebecca Berlin's grandmother, Gemma, often told Rebecca and her sisters an unusual version of the Sleeping Beauty fairy tale. Gemma identified strongly with the character of Briar Rose, but no one thought much of it until after her death, when a box of clippings and photos turns up. Rebecca decides to trace her grandmother's history and try to find the truth behind the fairy tale; her journey eventually leads to an extermination camp in Poland.

Children of the Blitz. Westall, Robert. 1987. London: Penguin.

This collection of nostalgic accounts from the eyes of the British who experienced World War II for themselves captures the mood of childhood from 1939–1945. The stories range from huddling in an air-raid shelter to searching for rationed food. Westall manages to depict the creativity and joy children can find in even the bleakest circumstances.

In My Father's House. Rinaldi, Ann. 1996. New York: Scholastic.

The McLean family of Virginia experience the Civil War in dramatic fashion from the beginning when they entertain Confederate soldiers on the eve of the Battle of Bull Run, which takes place on their property, to the end when the peace negotiations are held in their war-torn home in Appomatox. Throughout the war, Oscie, the narrator, learns to think for herself and develops a mutual respect and love for her stepfather Will who is as strong-minded as she is.

Machine Gunners. Westall, Robert. 1999. Minneapolis: Sagebrush Bound.

Night after night during World War II, the Germans rain bombs down upon Britain. Chas McGill and his friends collect shrapnel and other war souvenirs—the most valued being the machine gun they pull out of a downed plane. The boys hide the gun in a secret fortress, vowing to fight the Germans for themselves.

My Brother Sam Is Dead. Collier, Christopher, and James Lincoln Collier. 1974. New York: Four Winds.

Tim Meeker, growing up during the American Revolution, loves and respects his older brother Sam. Sam steals his father's gun and joins the rebel forces, while the boys' father remains loyal to the British. Tim must choose between the two sides and the two members of his family.

Number the Stars. Lowry, Lois. 1989. Boston: Houghton Mifflin.

Lois Lowry tells a fictionalized story from the real-life Nazi occupation of Denmark during World War II. As the people of Denmark organize to move Danish Jews safely to Sweden, ten-year-old Annemarie Johannesen and her family harbor Annemarie's best friend, Ellen Rosen, who is Jewish.

Steal Away. Armstrong, Jennifer. 1992. New York: Orchard.

Susannah McKnight shares with her granddaughter her story of flight to the north with the slave given to her when her parents die and she is forced to live with her aunt and uncle in Virginia during the Civil War. As a thirteen-year-old, Susannah believes slavery is wrong, and rather than treat Bethlehem Reid like a slave, she teaches her to read and asks her to help her return to Canada. On the long, dangerous journey that results in Bethlehem's freedom

and Susannah's return to the place she loves, the two girls become fast friends.

Summer of My German Soldier. Green, Bette. 1973. New York: Dial.

Twelve-year-old Patty's town becomes a camp for German prisoners during World War II. Patty, a Jew, shelters Anton, a young German prisoner who escapes, in a room above her family's garage. Her friendship with Anton grows as he treats her like a bright, compassionate young woman with important ideas to be shared. This humane treatment contrasts with her parents' ridicule and constant criticism and assuages the guilt she feels at betraying her family's good name in the town if Anton were to be found. Patty must deal with the consequences of her friendship within her family and her town.

The Clay Marble. Ho, Minfong. 1993. New York: Farrar, Straus & Giroux.

Thousands of Cambodian families were separated or destroyed by war in the 1970s. Dara's family is no different, but they have hope as they head for a refugee camp on the border with Thailand. After arriving at the camp, Dara makes friends with Jantu, who has a unique talent for making toys out of clay and scraps of fabric. Jantu gives Dara a clay marble that gives her the "power" to find her family and return for Jantu and her brother.

The Fifth of March: A Story of the Boston Massacre. Rinaldi, Ann. 1993. New York: Gulliver.

This well-researched story is about a fourteen-year-old indentured servant, Rachel, who is determined to educate herself. Rachel's position as nursemaid to the children of John and Abigail Adams during the period of time leading up to the Boston Massacre offers her opportunities to absorb the most well-reasoned arguments of the time regarding the impending Revolutionary War. As Rachel works to resolve her own feelings about war and humanity, she gains a social conscience and an increased sense of self-worth.

The Journal of Patrick Seamus Flaherty: United States Marine Corps, Khe Sanh, Vietnam, 1968. White, Ellen Emerson. 2002. New York: Scholastic.

Patrick rejects college for the Marines, and in December 1967 finds himself in Vietnam. His journal chronicles the loneliness, fear, developing friendships, and confusion he experiences during four months of incessant attacks by the Viet Cong at Khe Sanh. The journal is supplemented with a map, historical notations, photographs, and an epilogue.

The Keeping Room. Myers, Anna. 1997. New York: Walker.

When Colonel Joseph Kershaw leaves Camden, South Carolina to lead a Continental Army regiment in their struggle for independence, his son Joey, nearly thirteen, assumes responsibility for the household. When General Cornwallis chooses the Kershaw house as his headquarters and to the shock and outrage of the family begins hanging rebel prisoners in their garden, Joey must come to grips with his own sentiment about this war and any war.

With Every Drop of Blood. Collier, Christopher, and James Lincoln Collier. 1994. New York: Delacorte.

Fourteen-year-old Johnny lives in the Shenandoah Valley of Virginia during the Civil War. After his father dies while fighting for the Confederacy, Johnny, without his mother's permission to go to war, joins a crew attempting to get a wagon train of supplies to besieged Richmond. On the way, he and his family's mule team are captured by black Union soldiers. Johnny is forced to take orders from a boy his age, Cush Turner, and an unlikely friendship ensues, resulting in Johnny saving the Yankee's life.

Zlata's Diary: A Child's Life in Sarajevo. Filipovic, Zlata. 1994. New York: Viking.

Zlata Filipovic, living in Sarajevo, kept a diary from age eleven to age thirteen. She begins the diary with typical adolescent concerns about friends, school, and music. As time goes on, however, war consumes Sarajevo. Zlata's concerns turn to the constant bombing, lack of food and water, and deaths of friends and family members.

High School—Adult

All Quiet on the Western Front. Remarque, Erich Maria. 1929. London: G.P. Putnam.

Paul Baumer and his friends are part of Germany's Iron Youth during World War I, enthusiastic and sure of the justice of their cause and the glory of war. When Paul watches his friends suffer and die during trench warfare, however, he is changed forever. He vows to fight against the meaningless hate that causes war.

Catch-22. Heller, Joseph. 1961. New York: Simon & Schuster.

Heller's satiric work attempts to illustrate the absurdity and insanity of war. The plot involves the attempts of Captain John Yossarian to stay alive during World War II. Yossarian questions the logic of war, including the "catch-22" of the title, referring to an air force regulation.

Dispatches. Herr, Michael. [1977] 1991. New York: Vintage.

The author, a former Vietnam War reporter for *Esquire Magazine*, gathered years of notes from his experiences on the battlefield and turned them into what many considered the best account of the war to the date of its first publishing in 1977. He has captured the tone of the war and the essence of the people whose lives were changed by their involvement in it.

Farewell to Manzanar. Houston, Jeanne Wakatsuki. 1973. Boston: Houghton Mifflin.

The internment camp at Manzanar in the East Sierras in California was hastily constructed to house thousands of Japanese internees. Seven-year-old Jeanne Wakatsuki is taken with her family from Long Beach where her father worked as a fisherman. The author gives an account of her family's time in a Japanese internment camp. She discusses her life prior to being uprooted, during her family's internment, and after, demonstrating the resiliency of resourceful people to overcome fear and anger.

Hiroshima. Hersey, John. 1946. New York: Modern Library.

The author gives firsthand accounts of six people who survived the atomic bomb at Hiroshima. The author discusses the lives of the six subjects before, during, and after the bomb was dropped, giving a face to the atrocities and statistics of war.

Persepolis: The Story of a Childhood. Satrapi, Marjane. 2003. New York: Pantheon.

Satrapi, a descendant of the Emperor of Iran, recounts in graphic format the story of her own life during the Islamic Revolution in Iran. She presents a child's view of war without the use of sensationalism or sentimentality and succeeds in showing both quotidian life in Tehran and her family's pride and love for their country during difficult times.

Schindler's List. Keneally, Thomas. 1982. New York: Simon & Schuster.

The author gives an account, based on fact, of Oskar Schindler, a German who lived in Poland during the Holocaust. Schindler, an industrialist, constructed a "concentration camp/factory" to employ and hide Jews. He saved more than thirteen hundred Jews during the Holocaust.

The Red Badge of Courage. Crane, Stephen. 1925. New York, London: Appleton.

Henry Fleming, a Union Army soldier during the Civil War, dreams of glory. During his first battle, however, he flees in fear. As he faces his fellow soldiers, Henry begins to mature and realizes that war is not glorious. He becomes angry at the injustice of war but continues to fight as a truly courageous soldier.

The Things They Carried. O'Brien, Tim. 1990. Boston: Houghton Mifflin.

O'Brien tells a story about the Vietnam War through a series of interrelated stories. He tells the stories of the men of Alpha Company, including a character named after himself whose background and experiences are similar to the author's own. The stories depict the men's differing experiences during and after the war.

USING THE LITERATURE OF WAR THEME-SET

The book selections in this theme-set range from those that outline circumstances of war from the perspective of characters somehow involved in the conflict to contemporary remembrances of those lost in war. *My Brother Sam Is Dead* and *The Fifth of March* present opposing approaches to the development of consciousness about the difficulties of war. Both explore the sensibilities of the Revolutionary War, but Tim Meeker in *My Brother Sam Is Dead* blindly chooses the side of the Patriots because his brother, whom he idolizes, has run off to join their forces. The cognitive dissonance he experiences stems from his father's loyalty to the British. How is it that two men he respects can construct viable arguments to support opposing sides of a war? Rachel faces the same dilemma in developing her own identity and ideas in the face of the war in *The Fifth of March*. She witnesses the heart-searching discussions of John Adams and his colleagues as they struggle with whether or not war is eminent. Her friendship with a young British soldier further clouds the issue for her. Both Tim and Rachel must construct their own convictions about war as a component of life as they know it and apply its lessons to broader issues of life.

Several books grapple with the issues of the Civil War. Some like *Li'l Dan, the Drummer Boy, Pink and Say, Steal Away,* and *With Every Drop of Blood* portray the character of young people, both white and black, when faced with the circumstances of a divisive war. Personal experience on the battlefield changes the glorified view of war to the practical and grisly reality for some characters such as Henry Fleming in *The Red Badge of Courage*.

World War I is not well represented in the literature of children or young adults. The sole text of quality we were able to find, *All Quiet on the Western Front*, is often taught in high school classrooms today. Supporting this text with literature about the same themes from other wars would make a valuable contribution to students' understanding of the specific text itself and its message about war and its impact on humanity.

The treatment of World War II in literature of all ages is extremely varied. Some books approach it from the standpoint of hiding from the authorities such as *Summer of My German Soldier*, *Anne Frank: The Diary of a Young Girl*, and *Schindler's List*. *Number the Stars* is the story of the Danish people who organize to move Danish Jews to safety. Both of Robert Westall's books in the theme-set, *Children of the Blitz* and *Machine Gunners*, depict the lives of the British noncombatants simply trying to survive in a country torn apart by German bombs. The plight of Japanese Americans is represented by *Baseball Saved Us*, an account of life from the perspective of a child in an internment camp, as well as Jeanne Wakatsuki's memoir of her own internment experiences in *Farewell to Manzanar*. Survivors of the atomic bomb give firsthand accounts of their lives before, during and after the explosion in *Hiroshima*. Art Spiegelman's two-book set *Maus: A Survivor's Tale: My Father Bleeds History* and *Maus II: A Survivor's Tale: And Here My Troubles Began* are powerful graphic novels that translate the story of the author's father into a novel/comic strip reminiscent of Orwell's use of symbolism in *Animal Farm*. World War II is most strongly represented in the theme-set because of the selection of *Night* as the core text. In no way do we wish to minimize the significance of any other armed conflict. In fact some wars, most notably those that have devastated many African countries in recent years, are not represented because of the lack of easily accessible text appropriate to secondary students.

The Clay Marble and *The Journal of Patrick Seamus Flaherty: United States Marine Corps, Khe Sanh, Vietnam, 1968* paint aspects of the wars in Vietnam and Cambodia that permanently changed the face of southeast Asia. Tim O'Brien's firsthand account of the Vietnam War, *The Things They Carried*, when combined with the personal stories gathered by *Esquire* reporter Michael Herr in *Dispatches*, serve to differentiate between the controversial war and the soldiers who fought it.

In an effort to represent current conflicts, we have included *Zlata's Diary: A Child's Life in Sarajevo* that takes a similar approach as *Anne Frank: The Diary of a Young Girl*, but tells the story of another devastating war in Europe that is usually overshadowed by the study of World War II. *Persepolis: The Story of a Childhood* is valuable for several reasons: It is written from the perspective of a young girl in Iran during the Islamic Revolution; it explores some serious issues that are also prevalent in other Middle Eastern conflicts; and it is told in the genre of graphic novel.

Two of our children's books are touching tributes to family members whose lives were disrupted by war: in *So Far from the Sea* Eve Bunting's character pays homage to her grandfather who was interned at Manzanar, and in *The Wall*, another well-known book by Bunting, a boy and his father visit the Vietnam War Memorial to look for his grandfather's name. *Night* fits the category of remembrance in that Elie Wiesel could not bring himself to write about his horrific experiences until fifteen years after his release from Buchenwald, when he finally found the voice that would break his silence.

A dozen or more themes come to mind when considering the application of *Night* in the classroom. Because we want to focus on themes with which young people may most readily identify no matter what their culture, economic status, or familial circumstances, we will touch briefly on personal identity, loss, faith, and dehumanization that paralyzes the sensibilities of people in mind-numbing circumstances.

Personal Identity

Wiesel introduces the theme of identity in the opening sentence of *Night*: "They called him Moshe the Beadle, as though he had never had a surname in his life" (1). Having no surname is particularly problematic within Judaism and certainly suggests that his identity is in question. Wiesel is in jeopardy of losing his own identity despite of the retention of his name because his parents are gone, leaving him an orphan like countless other children he came to know, and his beliefs are in a shambles after what he believes to be the silence of God during the extermination of His chosen people. At the end of the book, Elie finally looks into a mirror: "From the depth of the mirror, a corpse gazed back at me. The look in his eyes, as they stared into mine, has never left me" (109). Can part of one's identity die? Has Wiesel lost a piece of himself? Can others impose an identity upon us? How do people come to view themselves if the world seems to attach no value to them?

One of the grave issues that disturbed Wiesel, both during his tenure in the camps and after the war, is that of the silence of the world. Before their exile from Sighet to the camps, the Wiesel family had been following the progress of the war via London radio news. Even though Moshe, who experienced the atrocities of the camps, returns to Sighet to tell the people to leave while they can, the villagers think he must have lost his mind. Surely there would have been some news of such an outrage as he describes. However, no corroborating information arrives, and the Jews of Sighet prefer remaining in their homes to emigrating to Israel or other towns or nations known to befriend them. Even after the war, many people preferred to discount the severity of the news about the concentration camps; it is more comfortable for us to look the other way when crimes are committed. Rather than confront our own humanity, we look away, and our silence chips away at the identity we have sought to develop. How does it change our identities to admit to the existence of genocide and not do everything we can to prevent it?

Loss

As a subset of the theme of identity, we may ask how does suffering and loss affect a person's sense of self? Psychologists define loss as that which "creates a gap between what persons have, want, or expect in life and what they now (at the perceptual moment of loss) get out of life" (Frost in press, 6–7). If we perceive ourselves as helpless in the face of adversity, we experience a gap between the events of our lives and our abilities to deal with them. The result is a sense of loss with which we may eventually come to terms. However, some losses are so great that our sense of balance in the world may never be fully restored. In order to restore some balance in our lives, we must be willing to accurately recall the moment of loss even though it is painful. Wiesel takes such a step at the end of the book when he looks in the mirror and describes what he sees.

A significant message to young people is not to succumb to the less painful state of denial. The villagers of Sighet hid in such a state saying, "Who knows? Perhaps we are being deported for our own good" (18). Dealing directly and honestly with loss is difficult, but it is the only way to move on with our lives.

Faith

From the beginning of the book, Elie Wiesel demonstrates his awakening adult awareness of Judaism by showing his emotional response to stories of past persecution, his interest in its history, and his insistent study of the mystical subset of Judaic wisdom, Hasidism, despite of the fact that such study results in his deviation from the path of the more pragmatic approach espoused by his father. Elie's faith is tested and even undermined by the death of infants and especially his anger at the prolonged hanging of the young boy too small to die immediately. He admits his weakness and confusion about feelings of disloyalty to his father when he tires of caring for an invalid who slows him down, and he doubts the mercy of a God who would allow such atrocities to happen. Even as he expresses his lack of faith, he reaches toward God for the strength to persevere.

Dehumanization

Many of the books in our theme-set deal with elements of dehumanization that seems by nature to be a common derivative of war. By taking away the humanizing attachments of civilization, such as our name and our personal clothing, and the vanity of hair and personal possessions, victims and prisoners in any setting lose essential aspects of their distinct humanity. People are often easier to control when they lose their dignity and, with it, their will to fight. As a member of the masses, individual will becomes subjugated to the whole. Wiesel is stripped and examined by soldiers who decide if he is sturdy enough to live and work in the camps. His head is shaved; he is decontaminated in the showers because Jews were thought to be carriers of disease; he is tattooed with the number by which he would be recognized in the camps; and he loses everything he possesses that is of any value to the trustees, even his gold tooth. He is of no consequence to his captors except by virtue of his ability to work. By caring for his father, he retains some semblance of humanity, but even that is in grave jeopardy as he contemplates allowing his father to die to alleviate his burden.

ACTIVITIES USING MULTIPLE INTELLIGENCES

Many tumultuous emotions revolve around us when we ponder or experience the trauma of war. It is these emotions we want students to consider when connecting the texts from a number of different wars in this set. The dates may change the technology or the motivation, but the experience of war is essentially the same when analyzed at the level of human experience. For this reason, the activities in this theme-set are organized around the themes themselves rather than milestones on a journey, as the previous theme-sets were.

Because of the events surrounding the attack against the World Trade Center in September of 2001 and later of the continuing war in Iraq, children today have a more realistic view of war and the violence that characterizes such conflict. Instead of viewing war from a fictionalized vantage point, children see color pictures on television, hear their parents discussing real people affected by violence, and are sometimes personally affected by war itself as they watch older siblings, parents, relatives, and acquaintances become embroiled in a nation's fight. Everyone is on the perimeter of tragedy, whether they are immediately or distantly affected. In working with this unit and to keep it from becoming one in which political sides must be chosen, participation in group activities and collaborative projects will allow the students to explore various affects of the literature of war.

Personal Identity

One way to begin working within the theme-set is to create an oral history project. Before giving students this assignment, we suggest teachers log onto a site, www.history.ucsb.edu/projects/holocaust/index.html, which gives a teacher's perspective on how to conduct interviews sensitively and with a purpose for the oral history. At the time of this publication, the University of California at Santa Barbara created and maintains the project and the site. The inspiration behind this particular oral history project is Nina Morecki, a survivor of Nazi genocide. Included on this site are links to provide students with interviewing questions, her life story, a timeline of events in Ms. Morecki's life and recommended current articles that will provide more information and inspiration.

During and after the creation of their own oral history project, students can use the material they collect as background for their own reading, as the basis for collaboration on a given theme, as the means to explore their own family histories or simply as the means to provide insight into the material they are reading within the theme-set. Later, their research can be "published" on a school or classroom website, displayed in a series for other classes, or used as a starting point for further research in related fields. (Linguistic, Interpersonal, Intrapersonal, and Bodily-Kinesthetic)

Loss

Though dealing with loss is never an easy subject for exploration, it connects all humans to each other because loss is as much a part of life as breathing. So, while students can immediately make the connection to Wiesel's *Night*, pairing it with another novel, *So Far from the Sea*, provides an intertextual extension. By studying these two novels together, the confusing concept of a "world war" becomes personal because students can see that one doesn't have to be *in* a war to experience loss of identity along with loss of respect and the loss of home as a refuge, all issues that arise out of this theme-set. Using her father's Boy Scout neckerchief as the literal tie that binds the narrator to her country as well as to her long-gone grandfather, the irony of the use of this purely American symbol is not lost on the reader.

During the previous exploration of the theme of personal identity, it was suggested that students conduct an oral history project, one that would result in the recognition of the reality of war. To continue this project, yet still deal with loss as the theme, have students also literally or figuratively collect symbols of their identities as members of a family, a social group, a club or organization, a school, a community, a state, a country, a nationality, a religion or belief system, and any other identity that makes them unique. In creating this collection, students are identifying who they are and what they believe. After creating this collection, they are to create a display that can be shared publicly on, say, a wall along with other displays, in an album, or in some other group display. Each item or picture must display a caption identifying the family or social group, and so on. As a final part of this symbolic description of who they are, ask them to do a five-minute quickwrite on losing access to all of their individual identifiers. In other words, ask them to define "loss of identity." They are to share their quickwrites with each other. (Linguistic, Spatial, Interpersonal, Intrapersonal, Musical, Bodily-Kinesthetic, Naturalist Intelligences)

Eve Bunting's *The Wall* has, from the beginning, echoed the power of the memorial to the Vietnam War. A person's name is his most basic and intimate possession as it carries meaning in its history, its connections to life, to family and to our "selves." Seeing his grandfather's name on the wall triggers a subconscious knowledge of the war and what it took from family. Using this book for the focus of a discussion, have students individually list the unanswered questions that arise from reading this book. Each question should be written on a half-sheet of paper. Putting all the questions in a shuffled stack, have each person take two or three to answer that night for homework. The reading of the questions and the answers written on the paper form the basis for discussion the next day. (Interpersonal, Intrapersonal, Linguistic)

Faith

Though *Schindler's List* might be familiar to students because of the movie, they will make further connections to the theme of faith as they read and recognize the same theme in Westall's *Children of the Blitz*, in Houston's *Farewell to Manzanar*, and Lowry's *Number the Stars*. Using the graphic Concept Map in Figure 5–1, ask students to explore the forms faith takes in each of the novels listed. After they have finished completing their graphics, ask them to come to a consensus as to a definition of "faith" as it applies to having faith during a war. (Spatial, Linguistic, Intrapersonal, Interpersonal)

Then, using their group definition of faith, ask students to individually apply this definition to examples from another novel of their choice from the theme set: Dividing their papers into two equal columns, have them list their

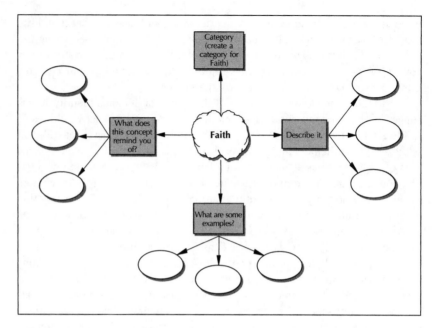

FIGURE 5–1   *Concept Map for Faith*

commonly agreed-upon definition of faith in the left column. In the right column, they are to list the examples of each aspect of their definition as it appears in the events or characters in the other novel they have chosen. (Spatial, Linguistic, Intrapersonal)

As a final task, ask them to write a two-page comparison of their versions of faith as they apply to war in one selected novel of their choice. They may use their two-column chart for their comparison. (Linguistic, Spatial, Logical-Mathematical)

Dehumanization

In this common derivative of war, students can partially identify with the stress the protagonists feel as they are deprived of possessions and a sense of their humanity. Have the students list the basic "rights" they believe all human beings (regardless of political, economic, or geographic status) should have. (These could be the right to perform basic life tasks, the right to exist, and so on.) Ask them to share their lists with each other within the group. If an example must be used to illustrate the task, remind students that in *Farewell to Manzanar*, the women placed paper bags over their heads to give themselves the illusion of privacy when they were using the gang toilets. The paper bags were an attempt to give themselves a measure of control over their own dignity. Then, ask them to consider how each protagonist in the novels lost control over his or her own humanity: How was each of the themes mentioned above (loss, faith, personal identity) shown in the novels they have read? Assign them the task of illustrating the scenes in the novels where dehumanization occurred. The illustrations, which are to be displayed, could be drawings, collages, a song, or a poem. Caution the students that they must exercise good taste in their choice of illustration. (Spatial, Intrapersonal, Musical, Naturalist)

To deepen the involvement with the theme-set, for each suggested activity students are given choices as to how they will interact. The value of the activities, however, lies in the power of the readers' synthesis of the literature of war. In such a powerful theme-set, students will come to see some realities of war with shared definitions and an expanded view of this literary theme.

6 | THEME-SET 4: THE BULLYING MENTALITY

Core Text: Lord of the Flies *by William Golding,* Great Expectations *by Charles Dickens, and* The Scarlet Letter *by Nathaniel Hawthorne*

Peer intimidation is not a new problem visited upon our teens, and it isn't only happening in prep schools where incoming freshmen are stuffed into garbage cans. Intimidation can take many forms. Colleges and universities are holding the line in the intimidation thinly disguised as off-campus parties or initiation to clubs or fraternal organizations. The fear of being bullied (or worse) is a daily experience in inner cities where the young would sometimes rather join a gang to gain a sense of belonging than face the intensity of life in a harsh environment. This problem is so rampant, ongoing, and historic that bullying is estimated to affect 15 to 20 percent of all students annually (Batsche and Knoff 1994). In fact, the National Youth Violence Prevention Center tells us that 5.7 million young people are involved in acts of intimidation, and their website www.safeyouth.org addresses the problem in great detail, even recommending twelve specific actions that victims or witnesses of intimidation can take to deal with bullying.

It should come as no surprise, then, that authors addressing the issue of intimidation find it easy to characterize incidents in such a way that their readers can readily identify with the literary situations portrayed. Reading about life-echoing situations, character's motivations, and plausible coping techniques provides a ready source for thought and discussion. We are each responsible for ourselves; religious and governmental conceptions aside, there is no big brother watching over us to provide a bulwark against intimidation. Any literature that helps us cope with life situations is literature that can give us dignity and self-worth in an increasingly difficult time.

To utilize this set, we are recommending that you choose one of three core texts: *The Scarlet Letter* (Hawthorne [1950] 1965), *Great Expectations* (Dickens [1861] 2001), and *Lord of the Flies* (Golding [1954] 1962). We have chosen these three because they span eras and represent both British and American literature. Depending upon the goals you set in using the texts, you might find, for example, that Golding's *The Lord of the Flies* works better for your selected theme. Or that *The Scarlet Letter* fits better into an American literature class using the historical periods as a curriculum guide. Should you wish to narrow the Bullying Mentality themes to be even more specific to focus on women's issues throughout history, *The Scarlet Letter* could be paired with *The Color Purple* (Walker 1982), which features a protagonist who, after suffering at the hands of the men in her life, parallels Hester's display of inner strength, enabling survival and prosperity of spirit. Also included in the Bullying Mentality set is Joyce Carol Oates' *Big Mouth and Ugly Girl* (2002) with a protagonist who becomes strong enough to veer away from others' judgment of her personal worth to become more than a beautiful spirit and important to the survival of another. This plays nicely with Eleanor Estes' *The Hundred Dresses* (1944) where a young girl's realization of her responsibility for another's suffering subtly allows the reader to reflect on his or her own real-life actions toward others. The books in this set may be grouped flexibly for maximum impact, depending upon the academic needs and demographics of the classes in which they are being used.

In all these core texts, limitless possibilities exist to create opportunities for writing, reflection, and inquiry, elements that bring about growth in critical thinking and the ability to bring new learning to life experience. This precept is at the heart of the theme-set design. As teachers we want our students to benefit more from the reading experience than simply having the means to pass high-stakes tests, though there is certainly that advantage as well. Students who can compare what they learn to life experiences and who can extend their thinking to situations they haven't yet experienced gain more in the ability to create new learning for themselves than they would derive by answering questions at the end of a chapter or by simply having a discussion about a single text. By law, teachers and parents step away from mandated mentorship by the time students graduate from secondary school. At the age of eighteen, students are generally considered adults in most legal situations. In the United States, they can sign contracts, vote in elections, join the military, serve on a jury, and become independent financially. As teachers, our task is to provide situations in which these future citizens can gain skills necessary to deal with adult responsibilities. This heady charge can be aided by the thematic concerns students come to consider. If the experience of working through a novel like *Great Expectations* is designed to offer those important skills, we as teachers must designed literature-aided lessons *for life.*

The oldest of the three texts is *The Scarlet Letter* by Nathaniel Hawthorne, first published in 1850. Set in early New England, this novel tells the story of Hester Prynne, who commits adultery with the young village minister and gives birth to a baby girl before the book begins. As a consequence of her act, Hester is condemned to wear a scarlet letter *A* for "adulteress." The child of this illicit affair is Pearl, a willful daughter who becomes the living embodiment of that scarlet letter. When Pearl's father, Pastor Arthur Dimmesdale, doesn't own up to his part in Pearl's existence, Hester's husband Roger Chillingworth, aware of the role Dimmesdale plays, capitalizes on the pastor's guilty despair and increases his torment and agony. Dimmesdale's suffering comes to an end, however, when he finally resolves to confess to his part in the earlier affair, and as he confesses his "sin," he dies. In this confession, he has also ended Chillingworth's obsession with tormenting the pastor. Chillingworth loses his grasp on the pastor at the same time as he loses his reason, and he also dies, leaving Hester and Pearl to survive and glory in their lives. Both victims of this Puritanical society have now become triumphant over the rules that originally kept them in shame.

Chronologically, *Great Expectations* by Charles Dickens is the next of the suggested core texts. First published in 1861, this text is a fairly accurate interpretation of several classes of society in Victorian England. The protagonist, Pip, is the embodiment of learning from "the school of hard knocks." First, Pip is victimized by life when he is orphaned. While living in a less than loving home with his sister and her husband, Pip visits his parents' grave and is approached by an escaped convict who bullies him into bringing him food. Magwitch, the convict, later reappears in Pip's life as his benefactor, but in the meantime, Pip's uncle takes him to a wealthy Miss Havisham, who sets him up for scorn and ridicule as a training ground for teaching Estella, a young woman being raised by Miss Havisham, how to break men's hearts. A naïve Pip falls in love with Estella, but we see that her mean-spirited behavior toward him belies her true feelings. Next, Orlick, a laborer working for Pip's brother, plays havoc with Pip at work and is suspected in the violent attack on Pip's sister. Life improves for Pip in the form of an anonymous benefactor (Magwitch) who provides funds for Pip's education, and as he indulges in the "high life," he rejects his family and earlier friends. Through a series of trying circumstances, Pip grows and matures, and eventually, he discovers his true benefactor is the convict. He assists Magwitch in an escape from pursuing authorities, but his assistance fails, and Magwitch ends up dying in prison, leaving Pip penniless. Pip reconciles with his family and years later, encounters a sad but now more realistic Estella. The reader is left with the possibility that Pip and Estella will continue through life together, even after all their earlier contacts were harsh and demeaning to both.

The last of the three core texts is William Golding's *Lord of the Flies* in which the characters are young boys who are stranded on Coral Island after a plane crash. It takes place during wartime, and the same warlike spirit raging in the outer world surfaces on the island as the boys form a tribe. Exhibiting behaviors originally designed to help them survive, the tribe turns their violent and warlike actions against themselves. Ralph and Jack, two older boys, come into conflict with each other. At first, they have separate roles. Ralph sets rules and encourages the boys to create a signal fire for any passing rescuers on ships or planes. But in their zeal, as they set fire to the pyre the surrounding trees catch the flames. After they have escaped the fire, the group realizes that one of the smaller boys has not reappeared. This is the first death. Jack, the hunter, leads his "choir" into the forest to find food, and though they are at first unsuccessful, their hunting trips eventually do yield a nursing sow, which they kill. That they could have let her live and raise her piglets for future food did not occur to them, but the death of the sow gives them reason to chant and dance around, an event that is the beginning of behavior more cultlike than civilized. Two more boys die, and the shocking behaviors of the group, including face painting, show how much they have descended into violence and loss of reason. They turn on Ralph and in howling pursuit of him, they run into naval officers who have come because of the signal fires they have burning. The irony of the ending is that they leave their warlike, un-civilized behaviors behind as they sail away on a ship destined for the war continuing to rage outside the confines of the island.

The following list for this theme-set is merely a suggestion of texts that could scaffold experiences with any of the three proposed core texts. The books on the list will lend themselves to many possible combinations, depending upon the nature of the themes chosen. The need to prevail over unjust treatment is a theme in all the selected texts, as is knowledge of self and survival through force of will. Including other texts to support and extend the learning is also possible. For example, Zora Neale Hurston's *Their Eyes Were Watching God* is a core text for another chapter, yet it would also serve as a core text with the previously mentioned feminist theme where strong female protagonists are required. In all the books within the Bullying Mentality theme-set, the means to cope with forces beyond individual control is a strong theme aided by the activities and goals selected.

THE BULLYING MENTALITY

Core Literature

Great Expectations. Dickens, Charles. [1861] 2001. New York: Dover.

Pip, a poor boy, begins to spend time with the wealthy, eccentric Miss Havisham and her beautiful, haughty niece Estella. Miss Havisham, who has developed a hatred of men, has taught Estella to feel the same way. Pip is led on and betrayed by Estella as he grows into a man with bright possibilities.

Lord of the Flies. Golding, William. [1954] 1962. New York: Coward-McCann.

When a group of English schoolboys are stranded on a deserted island after a plane wreck, they cooperate at first to find food and shelter. Ralph leads the boys, attempting to instill responsibility and order, but many of the other boys would rather fish and swim. The boys begin to rebel against Ralph's rules. Ultimately, the rebel Jack leads a group of boys to become a band of pig-hunting savages. Ralph and his friend, Piggy, become the prey of the rest of the boys. Typical adolescent struggles take on brutal, primal overtones.

The Scarlet Letter. Hawthorne, Nathaniel. [1950] 1965. New York: Bantam Classics.

Hester Prynne, living in Boston during the Puritan times, is forced to wear a scarlet *A* on her clothes after committing adultery and bearing an illegitimate child. When her husband, whom she thought dead, returns, he becomes obsessed with discovering the father. The father is revealed to be a guilt-ridden young minister who is at the forefront of those pressuring Hester to reveal the father. Hester's husband torments the minister, and the situation ends badly for both of them.

Picture Books

Enemy Pie. Munson, Derek. 2000. San Francisco: Chronicle.

The main character, a little boy, is upset when Jeremy Ross moves into his neighborhood. The two boys become enemies right away. The main character's father tells him he will cook an "enemy pie," guaranteed to get rid of his enemy as long as the boys first spend one day together. After playing together, the two boys become friends.

Hugo and the Bully Frogs. Simon, Francesca. 1999. London: David & Charles Children's Books.

Hugo, a small frog, is bullied by the bigger frogs in his pond. When Hugo meets a nice duck, he learns how to protect himself. The next time the bully frogs come around, Hugo frightens them with a loud "Quack!"

King of the Playground. Naylor, Phyllis Reynolds. 1991. New York: Maxwell Macmillan International Publishing.

Sammy appoints himself king of the playground and terrorizes others on it, including Kevin. After discussing the problem with his father, Kevin comes up with a way to outwit Sammy.

Odd Velvet. Whitcomb, Mary E. 1998. San Francisco: Chronicle.

Velvet is different from all the other children in her class. The other children tease and taunt her. When Velvet wins a school drawing contest, the other children finally begin to appreciate her uniqueness.

Shrinking Violet. Best, Cari. 2001. New York: Farrar, Straus and Giroux.

Violet is shy and wants to shrink every time Irwin, the class bully, teases her. With her best friend Opal, Violet's flair for humor and impersonations shines through. On the night of the class play, Violet sees Irwin in a different light when he forgets his lines. Rather than take revenge on him, Violet impersonates his voice and says his lines for him.

Stand Tall, Molly Lou Melon. Lovell, Patty. 2001. New York: G. P. Putnam.

Molly Lou Melon is small and awkward, but she has never minded because her grandmother has supreme confidence in her and urges her to have confidence in herself. When Molly moves away from her friends and grandmother, she must deal with a bully who makes fun of her quirks. Molly's self-confident attitude wins the day, however, and turns all her faults into talents.

The English Roses. Madonna. 2003. New York: Calloway.

The four little girls in this book do everything together. All four are jealous of Binah, whom they believe to be beautiful and smart. They are mean to her and ignore her until they find out that she is lonely and poor. A fairy godmother teaches them not to judge people by their appearances.

The Present Takers. Chambers, Aidan. 1983. London: Bodley Head.

Lucy goes to school with a group of girls who always get what they want. The group takes presents and money from their classmates and torments them if they won't give up their belongings. Lucy and her new friend Angus decide to stop them once and for all.

The Recess Queen. O'Neill, Alexis. 2002. New York: HarperTempest.

Jean is the recess queen at her school, and she torments those who get in her way. When a new student, Katie Sue, comes to school, things change. Katie Sue is not afraid of Jean and even asks to play with her. Before long, Jean and Katie Sue are friends, and Jean is not the bully she once was.

The Sneetches and Other Stories. Seuss, Dr. 1961. New York: Random House.

In *The Sneetches,* Dr. Seuss tells the story of two groups of Sneetches who don't get along. One group has stars on their bellies, the other group has not. The Fix-It-Up Chappie comes along and teaches the Sneetches that prejudice is pointless and harmful.

The Thanksgiving Visitor. Capote, Truman. 1996. New York: Knopf Books for Young Readers.

Capote, through his engaging characters from a previous book, *A Christmas Memory*, tells of the Thanksgiving when Miss Sook invites her cousin's grade school rival, Old Henderson, to Thanksgiving dinner. Buddy, the cousin and narrator, learns a valuable lesson about forgiveness and compassion.

Children's Chapter Books

Bad Girls. Wilson, Jacqueline. 2001. New York: Delacorte.

Mandy White is small for her age and is constantly picked on. Then she meets Tanya, the fourteen-year-old foster girl from next door, who is wild and fearless. With Tanya's help, Mandy feels as if she can face the bully who torments her the most; all that remains is for Mandy to learn to deal with bullies on her own.

Blabber Mouth. Gleitzman, Morris. 1992. Australia: Piper.

Rowena Batts has a disability that prevents her from speaking. She is teased by the class bully at her new school and embarrassed further by her eccentric father. She finally finds an ally at school who helps her confront her father.

Crash. Spinelli, Jerry. 1996. New York: Knopf.

In this book, the bully is the narrator, giving his side of the story. Crash Coogan has been bullying Penn Ward since first grade; in junior high, Crash is a star football player while Penn is a cheer-leader. Though Crash seems to have everything, Penn has two things that are more important—the attention of his parents and the admiration of a beautiful girl at school. After Crash's grand-father suffers a stroke, Crash realizes that there are more important things in life than tormenting others. Crash and Penn, united by their common bond of love for their grandfathers, become friends.

Dear Mr. Henshaw. Cleary, Beverly. 1983. New York: Morrow.

Leigh begins writing to his favorite author in second grade and continues writing to him for four years. In the letters (some sent to Mr. Henshaw, some kept in a diary), Leigh chronicles his troubles as the new kid in school, where his lunch is stolen every day, as well as his troubles at home.

Harry Potter and the Sorcerer's Stone. Rowling, J. K. 1998. New York: A. A. Levine.

Harry Potter, raised since his parents' deaths by his aunt and uncle, is bullied by his cousin and treated unfairly by his aunt and uncle. On his eleventh birthday, a mysterious giant named Hagrid finds Harry and tells him that he is a wizard; his parents were a witch and a wizard. Harry leaves for Hogwarts School of Witchcraft and Wizardry, where he is again bullied by Draco Malfoy, but he also finds true friends and adventure.

Loser. Spinelli, Jerry. 2002. New York: Joanna Cotler.

Donald Zinkoff has always been a loser, even though he is a great person. He giggles relentlessly, is clumsy, and gets bad grades, among other things. When he loses a race for his school's team, his classmates begin to treat him badly. He is taunted, ostracized, and treated cruelly. Through it all, however, Donald never loses his positive outlook.

The 18th Emergency. Byars, Betsy. 1973. New York: Viking.

The school bully threatens to kill twelve-year-old Mouse. Mouse finds little help from those around him and must prepare for the "emergency" alone.

The Girls. Koss, Amy Goldman. 2000. New York: Dial Books for Young Readers.

Candace is the most popular girl in middle school, and she is always with her clique of girlfriends. Maya, the newest girl welcomed into the group, is suddenly and inexplicably ostracized by Candace. The other girls follow suit. Maya struggles to maintain her friendships with the girls and to figure out what went wrong. In the end, Maya retains her true friends, and Candace continues to pick and choose her friends with seemingly no care for how it affects the other girls emotionally.

The Hundred Dresses. Estes, Eleanor. 1944. New York: Harcourt, Brace.

Wanda Petronski wears the same faded blue dress every day but tells her schoolmates that she has a hundred beautiful dresses at home. The other girls, who know that Wanda is poor, taunt her for this lie. To make matters worse, the town as a whole verbally abuses the family because of their Polish heritage. Maddie, one of Wanda's schoolmates, finally feels guilty for not speaking up against the tormentors. When she tries to find Wanda, she discovers that her family has already moved, and Maddie realizes the role she played in Wanda's leaving.

There's a Boy in the Girls' Bathroom. Sachar, Louis. 1987. New York: Knopf.

The other kids at school hate Bradley Chalker. He is bright and imaginative, but also lies and bullies. His insecurity causes him to be so unlikable that he even alienates one boy who reaches out as a friend at first. Eventually, the new school counselor helps Bradley to gain self-confidence and acceptance.

Young Adult

Big Mouth and Ugly Girl. Oates, Joyce Carol. 2002. New York: HarperTempest.

Ursula Riggs thinks of herself as Ugly Girl and has built up indifference to this fact. When Matt Donaghy is suspected of being a terrorist after making a joke about blowing up the school, Ursula defends him. Though he is cleared, Matt's friends desert him and his family receives hate mail. As the cruelty escalates, Matt considers suicide. Ursula stops him, and the two help each other as they become friends.

Give a Boy a Gun. Strasser, Todd. 2000. New York: Simon & Schuster Books for Young Readers.

Strasser presents a fictionalized, yet true-to-life, account of two harassed boys who have had enough. After being tormented by their classmates for years, Brendan and Gary decide to take revenge. Their shooting rampage at the school has tragic results for everyone involved.

Holes. Sachar, Louis. 1998. New York: Farrar, Straus & Giroux.

Stanley Yelnats is unjustly accused of stealing sneakers meant for a charity auction. He is sent to Camp Green Lake, where the boys spend all day digging holes in the desert. The boys are treated unfairly by the camp staff, including the frightening Warden, except when they find something in the dirt. Zero, another boy at the camp, is clearly the least popular; when he and Stanley team up, the other boys berate them both. The two eventually run away and attempt to solve the mystery of Camp Green Lake.

Hoot. Hiaasen, Carl. 2002. New York: Knopf.

Roy Eberhardt is used to being the new kid and being pushed around by bullies. Because of the bully at his new school, however, Roy meets two other kids—one of whom beats up bullies—who become his friends. The three soon find themselves involved in a mystery regarding endangered miniature owls.

Roll of Thunder, Hear My Cry. Taylor, Mildred D. 1976. New York: Dial.

Cassie Logan, an African American girl growing up in the 1930s, must deal with prejudice and racist attacks. Cassie and her brother face taunting and abuse from their schoolmates, and their family must deal with racism from adults in the town. The family tries to stay together and keep the land they own through it all.

Speak. Anderson, Laurie Halse. 1999. New York: Farrar, Straus & Giroux.

After Melinda calls the cops and busts a high school party, no one at school will speak to her. At home, her parents barely communicate with her, leaving sticky notes when they leave for work.

Melinda finds it harder and harder to speak and instead remains alone with her thoughts. When Melinda finally realizes the true reason for her muteness—a rape that occurred the night of the party—she finally finds her voice and confronts the rapist.

Stargirl. Spinelli, Jerry. 2000. New York: Knopf.

Stargirl has been homeschooled her entire life, but in tenth grade she begins attending the local public high school. She is not like her classmates; her unique and eccentric nature at first causes her schoolmates to be curious about her. When she becomes a cheerleader and imbues the school body with school spirit, everyone begins to adore her. Eventually, however, her popularity wears off as her schoolmates find out that Stargirl has just as much enthusiasm for the other team as she does for her own school's. Her former friends and admirers begin to shun her, and her boyfriend encourages her to conform. Though she does conform at first, she ultimately returns to her true self and eventually leaves the school. Her boyfriend realizes that it was a mistake to ask her to conform and that he lost her as a result.

The Chocolate War. Cormier, Robert. [1974] 2004. New York: Knopf.

Jerry Renault refuses to sell chocolate during his school's fundraiser, creating quite a stir. Although some agree with Jerry and view him as a hero, to others he is a scapegoat. Jerry is victimized and bullied by those who are running the fund-raiser; his struggle turns into a schoolwide fight.

Witness. Hesse, Karen. 2001. New York: Scholastic.

In 1924, the Ku Klux Klan infiltrates a small Vermont town. Some members of the town embrace the Klan's philosophy while others fight against it. Hesse tells the stories of different people who are affected by the Klan's arrival, including a black girl and her father and a young Jewish girl. When Esther, the Jewish girl, and her father are shot at, the town decides to take action to remove the Klan.

High School—Adult

Fences. Wilson, August. 1995. New York: Plume.

The story of an African American family living during the era of racial segregation, Wilson's play explores the painful relationships that exist when people do not listen to one another or share each other's dreams. Troy Maxson bullies his son Cory into submission and treats his wife Rose with disrespect. When his philandering results in the birth of a child by a woman other than his wife, Rose swallows her pride and forgives him, offering to raise the child as her own.

The Color Purple. Walker, Alice. 1982. New York: Harcourt, Brace, Jovanovich.

Celie, abused and raped by her father at age fourteen, tries to keep her sister from suffering the same fate. Unfortunately, she also marries an abusive man, Mister, who torments her and keeps her sister's letter from her. Many years later she finds her best self after watching the example provided by her friend's independence and love.

To Kill a Mockingbird. Lee, Harper. 1960. Philadelphia: Lippincott.

Jem and Scout Finch are growing up in a small Alabama town during the Depression. Their father, a lawyer, defends a black man against unfounded accusations of rape in a highly controversial trial. Jem and Scout must deal with the townspeople's prejudice against the accused and their cruelty toward Atticus Finch for defending him. Though the accused is found guilty, the father of the girl who was raped still tries to take revenge on Atticus for his part in the trial by attacking Atticus' children.

USING THE BULLYING MENTALITY THEME-SET

One unsavory aspect of human behavior, controlling others by intimidation, and the societies that give rise to this type of behavior are recurring literary subjects across both fiction and nonfiction books for all ages. We read in our morning newspapers about bullying behavior in schools and families as well as in the worlds of entertainment, sports, and politics. How much adversity can the human spirit endure? This is a question germane to all recommended books in this theme-set. In one, *Lord of the Flies,* the author leads us to believe that only the controlling influence of civilization keeps us from being savage to each other. The early American Puritans attempt to control human behavior in *The Scarlet Letter*, but the protagonist allows us to view the victims' ultimate victory over this puritanical rigidity. In all the recommended texts, various versions of intimidation/victimization provide the basis for discussion and examination of human behavior within three recommended themes: knowledge of self (as a means for survival); survival through force of will; and the need to prevail over unjust treatment. As teachers of literature, we can ably guide our students through the process of dealing with these themes with the assistance of thought-provoking, accessible material, such as that which these theme-sets provide.

As the issue of bullying activity and its consequences continues to be explored in popular media as well as text, variations in the story line arise. Film-makers often exploit the bully-victim theme in their film projects either as the main focus or as background for characters' motivations within the film. For example, we laugh at Ralphie's dilemma when he comes face to face with the school bullies in *A Christmas Story* ([1983] 2000); we also sympathize with his plight and his later fancy that his hero-self will vanquish his foes. This does not happen very often in life, so when it happens in literature, the rescuer (hero-self) must have established credibility and worthiness before the reader can accept the rescue as being realistic.

Knowledge of Self

In order for characters to be perceived by sometimes skeptical readers as capable and heroic selves, they need to mature through their adverse circumstances, growing in their self-knowledge and personal confidence. This is, in part, one reason why the character of Pip in *Great Expectations* endears himself to many readers despite his pompous, irresponsible stage. Throughout the book, he manages to overcome numerous slights, losses, and misfortunes through self-discovery. This theme is prevalent in many of the children's and young adult books in the set. *Shrinking Violet*, *Stand Tall, Mary Lou Melton*, and *Hugo and the Bully Frogs* all show what a difference it makes for young people to have a strong sense of self when standing up to adversity. Some books also show how the bully him- or herself can change for the better because of self-discovery: *The English Roses*, *The Recess Queen*, and *The Hundred Dresses* are such books. Sometimes the protagonist learns about the dark side of human nature and is able to move past it even though there is no improvement in his or her circumstances such as Candace in *The Girls* and Harry in *Harry Potter and the Sorcerer's Stone*. In both cases, the conflict is only temporarily resolved, and the knowledge of self gained by the protagonists will serve to strengthen them in future confrontations. Occasionally, books offer a view of the ideal resolution to a bullying situation: The characters in conflict find that they are not so very different and become friends. *Enemy Pie*, *Crash*, and *Big Mouth and Ugly Girl* have the bullies and the bullied teaming up to help each other.

Survival Through Force of Will

Another inspirational theme in this theme-set is survival through force of will. We see this theme more clearly exemplified in books for older children through adults. Mouse in Betsy Byars' book, *The 18th Emergency*, finds no help from those around him and must fight to survive on his own. Harry Potter and his friends use their individual talents and sheer force of will to make it through the traps on the way to the sorcerer's stone (*Harry Potter and the Sorcerer's Stone*). Stanley Yelnats in *Holes* and Celie in *The Color Purple* both triumph over physical adversity and the intimidation of others by their grit and tenacity. It is this same strength of will that enables both Pip and Hester Prynne to survive difficult circumstances in two of our core texts.

Similar in some plot elements to *Great Expectations*, Beverly Cleary's *Dear Mr. Henshaw* features Leigh who is the "new kid" in school. In both novels, the reader is a sympathetic bystander who sees but cannot "touch." Because we can see into both protagonists' lives, it's difficult not to wonder at the harsh treatment life hands both of them. However, in *Great Expectations* and in *Dear Mr. Henshaw*, the novels' conclusions leave readers to reflect on life and upon the resilience of young people who have experienced such tremendous change in their lives. Survival through force of will in both cases comes about from maturity and the passage of time.

Need to Prevail Over Unjust Treatment

Sometimes people are so incensed over unjust treatment of themselves that they are able to find the strength to fight back even when they are outweighed or outnumbered. Such is the case with Maya in *The Girls*; Melinda in *Speak*, who finds her voice after a year of suffering in silence, and Scout in *To Kill a Mockingbird*. Because Scout is so young at the time, she loses some of her childhood innocence when she faces the attitudes of the town toward Tom Robinson and her father, who attempts to defend Robinson against a racially motivated rape conviction.

Young people today are often surprised that life experiences they have as they mature are the same experiences that all young people have, regardless of the time period or geographical setting. For example, even though *Great Expectations* features an unfamiliar setting for most students, they see that Dickens' Pip suffers through rejection and embarrassment and later becomes his own source of strength through his inward resolve. Even if students do not identify with Pip due to Dickens' style and word choice, they can easily see Pip as being the subject of much unfair treatment, a judgment readers can easily make from their own observations. The same is true of Hester Prynne in *The Scarlet Letter*. In this novel, harsh rules and consequences in the Puritan society would be featured as human rights violations on the front page of newspapers today. Yet, in early New England, we see that though Hester Prynne initially embodies the antithesis of Puritan society's idea of purity, she wins respect and acceptance through her grace and good deeds, her compliance with her punishment seen as another means of dealing with unjust treatment.

Often individuals who are bullied form alliances with others who also see the treatment as unjust, and they fight the bullies together. This happens on a small scale in *The Present Takers*, *Blabber Mouth*, and *Bad Girls*. Sometimes in the need to prevail over unjust treatment, people make poor choices and end up involved in a physically violent altercation. Brendan and Gary take revenge on those who bully them by going on a Columbine-like shooting rampage at their school in Strasser's *Give a Boy a Gun*. In similar style, William Golding shows the darker side of human nature in *Lord of the Flies* when young boys are stranded on Coral Island during wartime. In the characters of Ralph and Jack, we see a descent into savagery and anarchy as they battle each other for control of the larger group of stranded boys. Initially battling over the importance of a signal beacon fire versus the importance of hunting for food, all the boys are catalysts for the deaths of Piggy and Simon, two of their number who symbolically represent good and reason. The group's cruel and thought-less actions foreshadow Piggy and Simon's demise, demonstrating how thin the veneer of civilization is. Unfortunately in life, the bullies sometimes win. This concept is somewhat echoed in Karen Hesse's *Witness*, where the Ku Klux Klan is only controlled after it has gone too far. However, in one novel, rea-son is absent while in the other, reason finally prevails because *Witness* attests to man's ultimate ability to use his humanity to control his baser instincts.

Another coping mechanism for some is to leave the circumstances behind. Wanda's family leaves town when their neighbors persist in tormenting them about their Polish heritage in *The Hundred Dresses*. Another young protago-nist, who has been homeschooled her entire life, enters public school in the tenth grade, only to find out that she will never be able to conform to the ideals of her classmates. She, too, makes the choice to leave the conflict behind (*Stargirl*).

The characters in the Bullying Mentality theme-set deal with bullying dif-ferently, some in an exemplary way and others with disastrous ends. All of them are representational of prevalent human choices and will provide much dis-cussion and debate. The following activities using multiple intelligences have been grouped somewhat differently from other chapters. Because we are sug-gesting three possible core texts in this set, the activities are more general to the discussion of the themes and may be adapted to any text. The first set of activities may be done as anticipatory sets or may be assigned while students are reading the books that preface or scaffold the core text. They represent a wide variety of intelligences and are designed to capitalize on critical think-ing skills that model making connections and facilitate self-learning. Later activities are more specific to the themes themselves. Where teachers need more direction in how to implement certain practices, websites or sourcebooks are listed that elaborate on the methodology.

Issues surrounding how humanity deals with harassment and even vio-lence at school, in the general public, and indeed, in the workplace have become fodder for discussion in every segment where such behavior is mani-fested. In fact, discussion is one of the ways we deal with issues that affect us, and we need only look at the popularity of such media as listservs or online discussion groups and the use of text messaging. "Americans care deeply about public life and civic culture—they just need to be invited into the conversation" (Moyers 1996, 14). So, we begin our activities in this set with conversation.

ACTIVITIES USING MULTIPLE INTELLIGENCES

Activity 1: What's Your Opinion?

Divide the class into groups of four or five. Each student within the group is to be given three statements with a corresponding Likert scale for each state-ment. (A Likert scale is a series of numbers that indicate a degree of agreement with the statement, from "strongly agree" to "strongly disagree".) These statements should generally state: (1) a description of bullies; (2) why bullies act as they do; (3) the best way to deal with bullies. Then, *before* discussing the statements within the entire group, each individual must rate the validity of those statements with a notation on their individual Likert scales. They will need to decide if they strongly agree with the statement, mostly agree with the statement, or strongly disagree with the statement. They will then discuss their *individual* responses to the questions and come to a consensus as to the *group's* rating on the scale. At the end of the discussion, they are to create group statements that fit the general statement or description of bullies, their motivations, and the best way to deal with these intimidators. (Logical-Mathematical)

Statements for response:

It is seldom effective to fight bullies.
Bullies cannot be retrained to be respectful of others.
The need for power is behind every bully's behavior.

Activity 2: Compare and Contrast

Based upon incidents of peer intimidation in the theme-sets, students create a Venn diagram comparing the actions and characteristics of bullies with the victim reactions and characteristics. This could also be in a chart form. (Logical-Mathematical)

Activity 3: Web Quest

Based upon the concept of bullying, students create a web quest in which they see all the books in the theme-set and explore links from each theme-set to links that lead to famous stories of the effects of peer intimidation (for example, the Columbine High School tragedy), the concept of retribution for such events (for example, movies featuring "payback"), the ripple effects of our actions and the actions and reactions of the characters in the theme-set, and so on. You will find everything you need to create a web quest at this site: http://webquest.sdsu.edu/webquest.html (Logical-Mathematical)

Activity 4: Categorizing and Labeling

Using the theme-set in its entirety and with the collaboration of a literacy circle of four, students will:

1. Create a list of all the occurrences of intimidation found in the sets.
2. Categorize and label each incident as to type of bullying, such as "psychological," "physical," and so on. (See the website www.safeyouth.org for more information.)
3. With input from the entire group, create a graphic or chart, naming and describing each category and listing representative incidents from the books in the theme-set. Leave space for a listing of other literary examples of this type of intimidation.

4. Each literacy circle member then selects one of the categories and writes a comparison essay, linking the examples from literature in the category to other examples of such behaviors. The comparisons can be from personal experience, current events, film, and other literary pieces or from a combination of any media. (Linguistic)

Activity 5: Interview a Psychologist

After discussing the incidents of bullying and effective (or ineffective) responses portrayed in each of the texts within the set, students create an interview in which a fictional psychologist or a panel of psychologists and an interviewer discuss the best methods to respond to and work with intimidators. This can result in a videotaped production or a live panel presentation to the class. (Linguistic)

Activity 6: Life-Size Representation

The class creates a life-size representation (like paper dolls) of the intimidator and the victim(s). This may not seem like something that would assist learning, but in both creating and viewing such representations, the characters become "real" to the students, and discussion is often more grounded. Angel Reed, a teacher in King City, California, adds a variation. To teach her students that their actions cause harm to others, she has the students create the life-sized figures, but they put names of characters on the figures. Each time students read of an action that bullies the character, students tear off a paper "body part," such as an arm or a finger. Then she has students write a letter of apology to the victim. Posting the letter beside the figure, students are told to tape the removed body part back on the figure. In viewing the patched figures posted on the wall, students catch the analogy: Though an apology might patch the character together again, the character is forever changed by the experience of being bullied (or offended). Students see the transfer of the lesson to life. When one of our student teachers assigned this activity in a seventh-grade class, she noticed a difference when students were on the basketball court at break. When someone called another student a name, other students would point and say, "Paper man!" Students said the activity made them stop to think about the insults that sprang to their lips in social circumstances, and when they thought before they spoke, they chose not to make the hurtful comment as readily. (Spatial, Linguistic, Intrapersonal, Interpersonal)

Activity 7: Color Symbolism

Using one of the websites devoted to color symbolism such as www.wired4success.com/colorsymbolism.htm, ask students to use color to depict the characters and scenes from the theme-set. They will need to write an explanation for the use of each color. The experience of assigning color (symbolism) to their character analysis is a lesson in inquiry because it requires the ability to compare in order to create new "meaning." (Spatial)

Activity 8: Illustration with a Caption

Students illustrate a crucial scene in the text and write the caption to be displayed for that scene. (Spatial)

Activity 9: Pay It Forward

Many schools require community service as a requirement for high school graduation. Thanks to this requirement, more teens are becoming aware of how their service affects others. Linking this social awareness to their reading, students should visit the Catherine Ryan Hyde website, www.payitforwardmovement.org/, on which the "Pay It Forward Movement" is featured. Assign the students to a group project, in which they actively watch and search for specific acts of kindness by teens who dedicate their actions to the concept of social change for the good of all. As the literacy circle also logs the events, plan on nominating one specific teen to the movement for honoring the activity. (Interpersonal)

Activity 10: Disasters and Traumas

In 2004 and 2005, a series of hurricanes struck the United States, across the Gulf Coast states of Florida, Mississippi, Alabama, Louisiana, and Texas. During this time, many homes and schools were either destroyed or severely damaged. People all over the United States collected and donated books and computer equipment to send to the destroyed or damaged schools so that students could begin to resume normal school life. Students may research current disaster or war-torn sites in need of resources in their quest for normal living and organize and participate in an effort to fill that need, either through collecting donations of equipment or through collection of funds dedicated to alleviating the need. (Interpersonal)

Activity 11: Survey and React

1. Students create an anonymous survey to be given to the class members. This survey asks class members what their experiences have been with intimidators and how they stopped the bully from harassing them.
2. Then they ask the same questions of teachers across campus (also anonymous), except they add an additional question: If you had a chance to be a child again, how would you stop bullies from picking on you?
3. Compare the results of the surveys and as a literacy circle group decide on the most effective way to stop harassing before it becomes destructive. (Interpersonal)

Activity 12: Values-Based Discussion

Ask students to think about and write a list of ten of their values that involve their interaction with other people and the world around them (for example, respecting the elderly). After they have created this list, ask them to write a letter to their future child in which they, the students, directly state which values they believe their child should have and practice. Ask them to explain why they believe in the values they state and what is the evidence of their actions in which this value is practiced. (Interpersonal)

Activity 13: Journal Entry

Ask students to write a learning log entry in which they discuss what they believe the causes of bullying are and what a possible plan might be to deal with peer intimidators. (Interpersonal)

Activity 14: Problem and Solution

Ask students to depend upon their knowledge of themselves and their skills to create a visual project that represents a problem one character in a book from the theme-set experiences. One component of their project should also be one solution that addresses that problem. (Spatial, Bodily-Kinesthetic)

Activity 15: Stomp Performance

After showing a clip from a video in which a "stomp" dance is performed, ask students to create their own stomp performance in which the characters from the theme-set interact with each other. (Musical)

Activity 16: Write a Re-creation in Poem

Students will write a poem in which rhythm and rhyme interact to re-create the story lines of two or three characters from two or three different books in the set. The poem could be humorous or serious. Students should be prepared to perform this poem orally. (Musical)

Activity 17: A Musical

Ask students to plan a musical based upon one of the texts they read from the set. Their musical must be at least one hour long and feature recognizable songs that are linked together with pieces of dialogue to tell the story. They are to write that musical to share with the rest of the class. (Musical)

Activity 18: Tableau Interaction

Give the following assignment to students who are eager to perform. In a group, students create a tableau in which two similar characters from different books in the theme-sets pose as if they were interacting with each other and with their intimidators. As students create the still life or tableau, they invite the audience to interview the characters. A variation would be to prepare an audience member ahead of time by assigning that person to the role of a victim (or bully) from another text. Ask that audience member to assume that role and to interact with the tableau characters during the live interviews. (Bodily-Kinesthetic, Interpersonal)

Activity 19: Tactile Lab

Three or four students in each literacy circle create a tactile lab in which they compare materials that the audience can touch with the emotions that bullies and victims within the text feel. For example, a bully might feel anger toward the victim. This could be represented by the touch of sandpaper. Label the psychological actions and reactions and invite the other students in the class to suggest other metaphorical materials that compare to the emotions you've represented. (Bodily-Kinesthetic)

Activity 20: Compare and Contrast

Students compare the behavior of territorial animals with the behaviors of the bullies in the theme-sets in a compare and contrast paper. (Naturalist)

Activity 21: Environmental Rationale

Have students examine the environmental context within which each character operates in the core text you've chosen to study. As a class you should create a rationale for the author's use of those specific environmental conditions to display behaviors of both intimidators and victims. (Naturalist)

KNOWLEDGE OF SELF

In each of the books within the Bullying Mentality theme-set, the protagonists must interact with or experience the effects of bullies' attitudes and acts. Overcoming such adversity often involves maturity and the realization that surviving intimidation involves knowing one's own strengths. Conducting role-based discussion literacy circles is an effective way to encourage the kind of dialogue that will focus upon characters' abilities to endure and triumph over intimidation by other characters, circumstances, and society.

In traditional role-based discussion groups, students are given roles to perform within the discussion (see *Literature Circles: Voice and Choice in the Student-Centered Classroom* by Harvey Daniels 1994). These kinds of activities involve students leading their own discussion groups and then making connections to the literature involved. This technique takes practice and some teacher guidance, though the discussions should not be led by the teacher at all. The teacher guidance is actually more like facilitating rather than monitoring, though that does need to happen when the discussion groups are first used. Students tend to let the teacher do the thinking for them if the teacher leads the group. The idea is to assist students in creating their own discussions within the stated parameters of their roles.

One variation of the role-based discussion group centers on a graphic organizer that everyone creates and uses as the basis for the actual discussion (see Figure 6–1). The value lies in the fact that the use of this graphic encourages inquiry and discussion, while at the same time, it takes the students through the process of formulating a question, supporting both aspects of the

Question **In choosing not to reveal his role in Pearl's birth,** **is Dimmesdale himself condemning Hester for adultery?**

YES	Commentary	NO
Because he is a minister, he is not being honest about his role! He preaches confession and repentance. He knows confession is good for the soul, yet he is committing another sin, the "sin of omission." By this new sin, he is condemning Hester as well as himself.	Perhaps in suffering he feels he is purifying himself, as if suffering atoned for the Puritan idea of sin.	If Dimmesdale were to admit his responsibility, he would lose the people's confidence and not be able to help anyone, least of all, himself. The greater purpose of his life role would not be served by confessing. More damage would be the result.
(more)	(more)	(more)

Evaluation/reflection:

FIGURE 6–1 *Graphic Organizer*

yes or no issue with information collected under columns detailing comparison ("yes") and contrast ("no"), allowing commentary space in the center of the graphic and culminating with drawing a conclusion. In making the "thinking" graphic, the process is facilitated in ways that appeal to the multiple intelligences involving spatial skills.

The final segment of the activity is an evaluation response where each student within the group reflects upon the group's conclusions.

One difficult aspect of role-based discussion groups is training students to listen and participate in the discussion while they are waiting for the chance to use their assigned role. In using this kind of compare-and-contrast graphic, students will scaffold on their discussions at the same time that they are creating the background material for later use, either as part of a written assignment or as another role in which they will all be participating during the role-based discussion. Additionally, by providing a defined space (the graphic) in which to channel their writing during discussion, students are being trained to negotiate what they say in the most specific manner. The other advantage of using this graphic is that by collaborating with the group in its formation, it becomes a nonthreatening, supportive way to structure their thinking into commentary, which is always a difficult skill to teach. (Interpersonal, Intrapersonal, Linguistic, Spatial)

SURVIVAL THROUGH FORCE OF WILL

Activity 1: Envelope Activities

The teacher creates five numbered envelopes for students to use in numerical order (and used once each session) in groups as they meet and work through the Bullying Mentality theme-set. It is advantageous for the students to begin to see how the characters in each novel are credible and that each novel has a basis in possibility. Teachers are often asked by their students why they have to read such books or what the reasoning is behind the book choice. It's not unusual for students to think that what they see as depressing literature is written by dysfunctional authors. Of course, we as teachers and readers ourselves know that sometimes literary works are written by such authors and poets just as some artwork and music is created by people who themselves could use some therapy. However, it is also advantageous for students to see that "normal" has ranges and that the characters they read about in *Lord of the Flies*, *Great Expectations*, and *The Scarlet Letter* could be real people. So, as you ask students to work through the Bullying Mentality theme-set, the numbered envelopes activity will serve to ground students to life and the possibility of parallels to life as they read. (Interpersonal, Intrapersonal, Logical-Mathematical, Linguistic, Bodily-Kinesthetic, Naturalist)

Envelope Possibilities

1. According to Louis Z. Cooper, President of the American Academy of Pediatrics, "10% to 12% of children and teens experience problems that need the attention of a mental health practitioner" (Cooper 2002, 76). According to this information, it is not uncommon for young people to experience life problems that they cannot solve on their own. Using the data below, figure out the exact number of students in each case who will need the help of a mental health practitioner.

   - There are 10,998 secondary students in our district. How many will need help?
   - There are 1,552 students enrolled in our high school. How many will need help?
   - There are thirty-four students enrolled in this class. How many will need help?

   Considering the numbers you have just derived from the above information, create and justify a statement about the need for this kind of help.

2. Using the storyline of the novel you are reading, do a three-minute quickwrite in which you draw a parallel with the excerpt of this lecture. Share it with your group. (Linguistic) The excerpt below is from Kofi Annan's Nobel acceptance lecture:

> In every great faith, and tradition, one can find the values of tolerance and mutual understanding. The Qur'an, for example, tells us that "We created you from a single pair of male and female and made you into nations and tribes, that you may know each other." Confucius urged his followers: "When the good way prevails in the State, speak boldly and act boldly. When the State has lost the way, act boldly and speak softly." In the Jewish tradition, the injunction to "love thy neighbor as thyself," is considered to be the very essence of the Torah. (Annan 2001)

3. Using the Annan quote again, answer the following question: How does this quote apply to the theme of survival through force of will in the novel that you are reading? Using a two-column graph, on the left list at least three points from the above quote and in the right column make or deny the connections point by point with your view of the situation in the core text. Be prepared to discuss your viewpoint in your literacy circle. You have five minutes to create your response. (Spatial, Linguistic, Intrapersonal)

4. The quotation below could be used in several ways in comparison with the texts in this theme-set.

> The dream we must now seek to realize, the new human project, is not "security," which is impossible to achieve on the planet Earth in the latter half of the 20th century. It is not "happiness," by which we generally mean nothing but giddy forgetfulness about the danger of all our lives together. It is not "self-realization," by which people usually mean a separate peace. There is no separate peace. . . . The real project is to realize that technology has married us all to each other . . . that until we are more courageous about this new marriage— ourselves all intertwined—there will be no peace and the destination of any of us will be unknown. . . . Men and women, black, brown, yellow, white, young and old . . . we must go wherever it is we are going together. There is no such thing as being alone. If we are the only one in the room, it is still a crowded room. But we are all together on this planet, you, me, us: inner, outer, together, and we're called to affirm our marriage vows. (Moyers 1996)

Activity 2: The Sequential Roundtable Alphabet

For this activity, all students need a copy of the Sequential Roundtable Alphabet (SRA) (Buehl 2001). To make one, they need to use a whole sheet of plain white paper. On this paper, they create a grid of one-inch squares so that they can place one letter of the alphabet in each square. (They will have to use the entire sheet for this.) After they have finished creating the grid, they will have two minutes in which they individually fill in the grid with a word, a term, or a plot element from the novel you are reading. (Set the timer!) For example, in the M box (if you are reading *Great Expectations*), they might place the term *moral theme*. Or for *Witness*, they might write "Ku Klux Klan" in the K box. Students should fill in as many boxes as they can, but it is alright to leave some blank.

When students are finished with the SRA, they should compare their entries with the entire group. For those in the literacy circle who do not know why a student used a particular entry, he or she should explain his or her reasoning. How does it connect with the selected theme? It's OK to share entries for the same novel *or* for those novels that have similar events occurring within them. After this activity is finished for all, students should use their SRA as a prompt as they continue reading throughout the rest of the novel. (Spatial, Linguistic)

Activity 3: Atmosphere (Tone)

Using the core text, students select a particularly well-written scene and complete the following.

- Select ten words from the scene that carry strong meaning or accurate description and that are appropriate for the theme you've chosen.
- Then, divide a paper into two columns. Put the words you have chosen in the left column. In the right, explain how the word fits the atmosphere (teachers call it "tone") of the scene.
- Then share with your literacy circle group.
- Compare the words and explanations for those words with the words and explanations that your literacy circle group has chosen. What is similar? What is different?
- Considering the words that your entire literacy circle has chosen, collaborate on a sentence that could be used to describe the atmosphere or tone of the theme-set books you are all reading.

Note to the teacher: This last activity could be used as a warm up to the discussion group work focusing on theme. (Spatial, Linguistic, Interpersonal)

Activity 4: "Half-Hanged Mary"

During the 1680s in Salem, Massachusetts, any woman who wished to live independently was viewed with suspicion. Sometimes, these women were persecuted or, in the case of Mary Webster, hanged. Her story is told in poetic form by Margaret Atwood in "Half-Hanged Mary" (1997). Mary survived her hanging and lived another 14 years. Read the poem in your literacy circle. Create a reader's theater and perform the story. Or, based upon Atwood's poem, create and perform a brief script for the reader's theatre. (Linguistic, Musical, Spatial, Bodily-Kinesthetic, Interpersonal)

THE NEED TO PREVAIL OVER UNJUST TREATMENT

Because this theme is often explored in literature, there is opportunity here for activities that will involve reasoned discussion, the kind that results from personal experience and not merely from some "research" that students are assigned. There are questions that occur in reading any text, and often, they are at the heart of what students learn by reading the text itself. On a bulletin board, create a display on which students may post unanswered questions. As the teacher, you will need to model some representative questions for them by creating a question yourself and posting it. For example, one such question could be: "Is the Beast something created by the boys to explain why terrible things are happening there? (*Lord of the Flies*)." Place paper and a pencil on the board for students to post their answers and other questions. By having the board visible throughout the readings, you will find that students post questions and responses on their own.

This type of format is easily duplicated on an electronic discussion board where students post questions and answers online. One such discussion board host is www.ezboard.com, and though there is a charge for its use, the fee is nominal for the months it would be used for your class. Of course, you yourself will wish to participate and monitor its use. Setting the norms for the electronic discussion board will be necessary, and you will also wish to agree upon how often students are to participate in discussions. There are other discussion boards that your district or county office technical experts can assist you in finding and using. Regardless of whether you use a discussion bulletin board or an electronic discussion list, the main idea is to draw students into discussions with the novelty of the presentation. Either way you use them, discussion lists and discussion boards are useful for giving students the means to discover what they know, how they can use what they know, and how what they know can lead them to new discoveries. (Linguistic)

Another technique to draw students into literature is to appeal to their personal exposures to the concepts being discussed or the focus of the texts. Almost all students have experienced some form of bullying, or if they have not, they have heard about or witnessed this behavior committed by someone else on another person. Because this is a shared behavior to which all have been exposed in one form or another, opinions are not hard to find among the students reading the theme-set. This is a subject designed for comparison. Ask students to participate in a Socratic-style discussion based upon the following statement: "Bullying is motivated by either fear or greed."

Guidelines for Socratic discussions generally involve having students first respond to the question individually, writing down the answer so that they have a stance on the issue. (It is advisable to have the students create their written response first because it allows them think time, during which their stance or response may be more articulately formulated.) Have half the students sit in chairs within a circle and include two "hot seats" on opposite sides of the circle. Socratic discussions have a greater chance of successfully involving all within the circle if you hold the numbers participating in the inner circle to fifteen. Arrange the rest of the class as silent observers encircling the discussants. It works well for the observers to keep notes on the speakers and their statements so that if the observers wish to participate, they may do so temporarily, joining the discussion circle in a hot seat long enough to pose the statement, listen to the response, and then reseat themselves in the outer observing circle. To begin, all the participants (including the teacher) need to be seated so that they have an unobstructed view of the entire circle. The teacher opens the discussion by making the statement again. The discussion is opened by having the student seated to the teacher's left create a response from what she or he has prewritten. Students will continue around the circle by either commenting upon the original statement ("Bullying is motivated by fear or greed") or by commenting upon one of the other discussants' statements. Because this is not a debate and the purpose is to open up thinking to new ideas, students should be forewarned to practice polite behaviors toward all. Often, as the discussion is nearing the end of the class period, teachers need to draw the discussion to a close by recapturing the idea of the responses or by asking for the outer circle (the observers) to comment upon the discussion itself in the form of a written reflection. Note the names of the inner-circle participants and make sure to exchange them with students from the outer circle in the next Socratic seminar.

At the conclusion of the seminar, ask students to write a reflection on the activity. This reflection should address what assumptions they had before the seminar, what has changed in their thinking, and what has stayed the same. To help them get started, have them create a list of their assumptions in a three-column format, with the headings: Initial Assumptions, What Has Changed, and, What Has Stayed the Same. Then have them write their reflection based upon what they wrote in their three-column graphic organizer.

Reflection could also take the form of a discussion of the quality of the responses. Students may also write about the connections to other pieces of literature they have read or movies they have seen. This is the best kind of commentary as the technique of comparing is a strong way of displaying how what they have learned is built upon "old" understandings. One form of written reflection is a Venn diagram, on which students are asked to compare "old" learnings with "new" or to compare an idea brought out in the discussion with a facet of the literature. (Spatial, Linguistic, Logical-Mathematical, Interpersonal, Intrapersonal)

All the activities in this theme-set can be modified to address state standards, to suit the size of the group, or to fit within the class period time frame. Similarly, the themes chosen for the focus of the activities may not be the only themes a teacher wishes to emphasize. Knowledge of self, the need to prevail over unjust treatment, and survival through force of will are only suggested themes. All the core texts have strong characterization and carry many moral and philosophical implications for today's reader. It only takes planning and delivery to make the texts "real" for students.

7 | THEME-SET 5: UTOPIAN/ DYSTOPIAN SOCIETIES

Core Text: Fahrenheit 451
by Ray Bradbury

The popularity of Michael Moore's politically charged film, *Fahrenheit 9/11* (2004), during the 2004 presidential election has caused a resurgence of interest in *Fahrenheit 451*, a classic dystopian novel by Ray Bradbury (1967). Ninth- and tenth-grade English teachers across America have reinfused their curriculum with concepts of censorship, government control, and personal responsibility for one's beliefs and actions. When rereading Bradbury's novel while searching for core books appropriate for our theme-set process, we found the plot details to be even more relevant today than they were when we taught the book fifteen years ago. The inclusion of a science fiction book at the core of one of our sets is also appealing as many high school students favor this genre. With the multitude of inventions made available by the scientific community since 1953, the year of publication of *Fahrenheit 451*, much of the science fiction of the book has become societal reality, if not in substance then on paper. Walls of television screens and robotic creatures do not even require a stretch of the imagination. Additionally, one need only have witnessed the televised broadcast of the initial phase of the U.S. forces' "shock and awe" campaign over Baghdad in March of 2003 to be able to hear and see the results of the type of war being waged at the end of Bradbury's book and to imagine the Herculean effort needed to rebuild a society destroyed by such an act.

Fahrenheit 451 is a book about a futuristic American society in which firemen start fires rather than put them out. People do not enjoy nature, and their social interactions are shallow and meaningless because books as well as independent thought are forbidden. They drive fast and are controlled by the media that constantly surrounds them from their wall-sized television sets to the "seashell radios" that are attached to their ears. In fact, these citizens are more likely to think of television characters as their close companions or family than their own spouses or offspring.

Through an encounter with a sensitive seventeen-year-old girl, Guy Montag, a fireman and the protagonist, begins to see the emptiness of his own life. After a series of upsetting events, Montag becomes increasingly dissatisfied with his life and seeks the answers in some stolen books. He seeks help from a retired English professor, Faber, in understanding what he is reading. Montag's wife is disturbed that he is reading books and reports him to his own fire chief, Beatty, who forces him to burn his own home. After Montag turns the flamethrower on Beatty and kills him, with Faber's help he runs away from the city and the mechanical dog Beatty had programmed to kill him.

During his escape, Montag floats down the river wearing Faber's clothes to disguise his scent. In the country he follows a set of abandoned railroad tracks until he meets up with a group of outcast intellectuals who are led by a man named Granger. They are called the "Book People" because they have collectively memorized many of the great works of literature and philosophy. Montag joins them and is assigned the job of memorizing the "Book of Ecclesiastes." War is declared in the city, and the Book People hope to find survivors of the blanket bombing that has darkened the sky and to rebuild their world, including in it the valuable experiences recorded by famous writers and thinkers of the past.

The following list of utopian/dystopian literature contains many books with which students may be familiar. The genres of children's and young adult literature abound with texts that present alternate worlds that follow their own rules and conventions. In fact, children's books in general reveal a utopian tendency that stems from a longing for a better world, argues Jack Zipes (Hintz and Ostry 2003, ix). Children need the hope that utopian literature offers them; therefore, elements of what Lyman Tower Sargent calls "social dreaming" are prevalent in most children's literature (qtd. in Hintz and Ostry 2003, 2). We have not annotated some of the most readily recognized examples of such, but we do want to mention here the vast array of books in the Dinotopia series by James Gurney, the highly popular Harry Potter series with its tales of Hogwarts, and Madeline L'Engle's classics *A Wrinkle in Time* (1962), *A Wind in the Door* (1976), and *A Swiftly Tilting Planet* (1978). Any texts that raise questions about political organizations and an ideal society that focuses on the built rather than the natural world could be considered utopian/dystopian literature.

UTOPIAN/DYSTOPIAN SOCIETIES

Core Literature

Fahrenheit 451. Bradbury, Ray. 1967. New York: Simon & Schuster.

Montag, a fireman in a futuristic world, follows the dictates of his superiors, who are trying to control independent thought by burning books. When he makes an escape from "civilized" society, he finds a culture of people who value books and have each committed a book to memory to preserve them for future generations.

Picture Books

Aunt Chip and the Great Triple Creek Dam Affair. Polacco, Patricia.
1996. New York: Philomel.

Aunt Chip, the town librarian, takes to her bed when Triple Creek
builds a huge television tower, predicting that there will be dire
consequences. Fifty years later when people are obsessed with
television and use books only as roof patches and furniture props,
Aunt Chip rebels and teaches the town children to read. The
children are so eager to find books that Aunt Chip's nephew and
his friend snatch a copy of Moby Dick from the hole it's been
plugging up in the dam. The resulting wall of water, floods the
town and destroys the TV tower, changing the town's future. When
the people of the town are enslaved by television, the illustrations
are dismal and gray and the town is imprisoned by power lines.
After the "release" from technology, the town comes back to life.

Babar the King. Brunhoff, Jean de. 1935. Translated by Merle S. Haas.
New York: Random House.

Most young people will recognize Babar from their early reading
experiences. In this book, King Babar rules over his kingdom from the
utopian capital Celesteville where all citizens are productive and happy.
Winged elephants chase away any misfortune that befalls the city.

Richard Wright and the Library Card. Miller, William. 1997. New York:
Lee and Low.

Acclaimed African American author of *Black Boy* and *Native Son*,
Richard Wright, finished his formal education in the ninth grade
but received his inspiration to write from having gained access to
the public library due to the efforts of a white coworker. This book
shows how the power of determination can make a dream a reality.
It's a nice complement to the themes of censorship and the fear of
knowledge that run throughout *Fahrenheit 451*.

Roxaboxen. McLerran, Alice. 1990. New York: Lothrop, Lee & Shepard.

Marian, her sister, and their friends create an imaginary world from
old wooden boxes, cactus, and greasewood on a sandy hill covered
with rocks. They believe it is a world of sparkling, bejeweled
homes and two ice cream shops that flank streets lined with
beautiful white stones. This book is a triumph of imagination.

The Rebellious Alphabet. Diaz, Jorge. 1993. New York: Henry Holt.

Placido foils the plans of an illiterate dictator who bans reading,
writing, and printing in his village when he attaches letters of the

alphabet to the feet of seven canaries who hop from inkpad to paper until a piece of writing is complete.

Weslandia. Fleischman, Paul. 1999. Cambridge, MA: Candlewick.

Wesley, a boy who does not fit in, plants a garden during his summer vacation and produces a crop of huge, strange plants that provide him with clothing, shelter, food, and entertainment. He creates his own language and counting system, uses a flower stalk as a sundial to tell time, and invents sports that rely on strategy and complicated scoring systems. Soon his classmates who once tormented him become curious and want to participate in this idyllic world.

Where the Wild Things Are. Sendak, Maurice. 1963. New York: Harper & Row.

This classic favorite of children everywhere tells the story of Max, who is punished for his wild behavior and is sent to bed without his supper. He dreams of an imaginary world where only wild things live, and he is crowned king because he is the wildest thing of all. His utopian, rumpus-making world becomes lonely without his family, and when he wakes up, he is happy to be home. Not only does he learn a lesson about valuing home, he also finds his hot supper waiting for him.

Children's Chapter Books

Charlie and the Chocolate Factory. Dahl, Roald. 1964. Illustrated by Quentin Blake. New York: Knopf.

Five children tour a chocolate factory run by Willy Wonka. It is full of unique inventions and an unending supply of tasty treats. The children meet the Oompah-Loompa workers and find out about Willy Wonka's vision for the future. The poorly behaved children are weeded out, and Charlie alone remains to inherit the enterprise.

Harry Potter and the Sorcerer's Stone. Rowling, J. K. 1998. New York: A. A. Levine.

Harry Potter, raised since his parents' deaths by his aunt and uncle, is bullied by his cousin and treated unfairly by his aunt and uncle. On his eleventh birthday, a mysterious giant named Hagrid finds Harry and tells him that he is a wizard; his parents were a witch and a wizard. Harry leaves for Hogwarts School of Witchcraft and Wizardry, where he is again bullied by Draco Malfoy, but he also finds true friends and adventure.

Maudie and Me and the Dirty Book. Miles, Betty. 1980. New York: Knopf.

When Maudie Schmidt and her friend Kate become involved in an interschool reading project, a small, quiet Massachusetts town is turned on its head.

Off the Road. Bawden, Nina. 1998. New York: Clarion.

In the year 2035, Tom and his grandfather, Gandy, live in a walled community where only one child is allowed per family and the old are sent to "Memory Theme Parks." When Gandy escapes the city, Tom follows him and finds another society that has its own problems. He searches for a way to balance the two systems.

Peter Pan. Barrie, J. M. [1911] 2000. New York: Simon & Schuster.

This classic tale presents one view of a perfect world as a place where one need never grow up and can have all the exciting adventures a heart could desire. As in all utopian tales, there is a downside, the loss of a true love. Life is, after all, a series of trade-offs.

The Secret Garden. Burnett, Frances Hodgson. [1888] 1998. New York: HarperTrophy.

When Mary is forced to move to England and live with her uncle, she discovers a walled garden that has been neglected for ten years. She and her cousin create a utopian space that brings them both the healing they need and even affects the adults in their world. This edition benefits from the classic illustrations of Tasha Tudor.

Young Adult

But We Are Not of Earth. Karl, Jean E. 1981. New York: Dutton.

A seemingly utopian "school/home" on the planet Meniscus F is for children who have been orphaned and exiled from Earth. Romula Linders and three of her friends are chosen for a mission to a new planet where they find the most perfect utopian world they could ever imagine until mysterious creatures attack.

Feed. Anderson, M. T. 2002. Cambridge, MA: Candlewick.

A brilliantly ironic and somewhat chilling satire, *Feed* is set in a future world where society is dominated by the feed of a next-generation computer/television hybrid that is connected directly into people's brains when they are babies. It provides a parody of teen-speak and style and a fast-paced world of conspicuous consumption. Titus, one of the vapid members of this society, finds that other options for life exist when he and his friends visit Mars.

With little help from his parents who are as empty-headed as he is, Titus begins to overcome his denial of the truth. (Profanity)

Gathering Blue. Lowry, Lois. 2002. New York: Laurel Leaf.

The companion novel to Lowry's *The Giver* (see entry p. 110), this book is set in a village with little technology and people who exemplify the most detestable of human traits: greed, envy, anger, and casual cruelty. Unfeeling authorities govern with an iron fist. Kira, an orphan who has been lame since birth, is an expert at embroidery and is given the task of restoring the historical pictures on a ritual robe. In doing so, she discovers a past that is also worth restoring.

Ice [*The Wintering*]. Bowkett, Stephen. 2001. London: Dolphin.

When the ice age destroys the world, a few thousand people find their way into the Enclaves, a series of shelters inside mountains and underground where they are governed by All Mother. In order to promote harmony, the weather is controlled; individual choice is nonexistent; and children never know the identity of their birth parents. As the thaw begins, people will want to return to the world and repopulate it, but All Mother has different plans.

Invitation to the Game. Hughes, Monica. 1990. New York: Simon & Schuster.

In the year 2154, high school graduates are either assigned jobs or are relegated to the unemployed. Ten students who do not receive a job assignment stumble upon what they believe to be a game but ends up being the government's way of colonizing other planets with their own young people. The story of their ability to work together to create a primitive but satisfying existence reaffirms the true necessities of life.

Messenger. Lowry, Lois. 2004. New York: Houghton Mifflin.

Matty lives in a utopian village that has prided itself on its welcome to new strangers, especially those who are disabled. He is disturbed by changes he sees coming, most particularly the closing of the village to outsiders. Being a gifted healer, he must decide whether to use his power to prevent the further decline of his community, knowing that such a move could be self-destructive. The gifted young people in *The Giver* and *Gathering Blue* come together in a final shocking scene that is sure to provoke much discussion.

No Kidding. Brooks, Bruce. 1989. New York: Harper & Row.

The author introduces readers to a world that has changed little from contemporary society except for the fact that some specific extremes are emphasized. The fourteen-year-old protagonist, Sam, places his younger brother with a foster family after having his mother committed to a treatment center for alcoholism. His father, who is a member of an extreme religious organization, is no help to Sam, and handling all of the adult responsibilities in his life forces him to grow up too quickly. This book focuses on the complexities of human nature we are faced with no matter what kind of world we create for ourselves.

The Day They Came to Arrest the Book. Hentoff, Nat. 1982. New York: Dell.

Barney Roth, the editor of his high school newspaper, decides that a solid piece of investigative reporting on past instances of censorship at his school will make a difference when a vocal group of students and parents want *The Adventures of Huckleberry Finn* (Twain 1948) removed from the school curriculum and the library.

The Giver. Lowry, Lois. 1993. Boston: Houghton Mifflin.

In a perfect world where there is no poverty, sickness, or unemployment, Jonas, the twelve-year-old protagonist, is chosen to be the Receiver of Memories of his community. Unfortunately, in order to create their "stable" community, its members have given up their humanity, including the differences that make us each unique. Jonas is faced with the choice of staying in his "perfect" world or leaving to search for the place he discovers in his newfound memories of the past.

High School—Adult Books

1984. Orwell, George. [1949] 1990. New York: Signet.

George Orwell's dystopian London may well have passed us by in the sequence of time, but the warnings about totalitarian control are as timely as ever. Winston is in grave danger because he realizes the Party controls people by feeding them lies and the Big Brother is watching him. He joins a revolutionary organization and with Julia, the woman he loves, decides to fight the powers that be.

Animal Farm. Orwell, George. [1945] 1996. New York: Harcourt, Brace.

This classic fable of a workers' revolution that does not turn out the way they had planned stems from Orwell's negative perceptions of Soviet Communism. The animals on Manor Farm overthrow their drunken human master and live well for one short season before the pigs begin to rule in much the same way as the human, twisting the Seven Commandment credo to fit their own craving for power.

Brave New World. Huxley, Aldous. 1946. London: Harper and Brothers.

In the "brave new world," universal happiness has been achieved (well, almost). Control of reproduction, genetic engineering, conditioning—especially via repetitive messages delivered during sleep—and a perfect pleasure drug called "Soma" are the cornerstones of the new society. It espouses the idea that contentment is more important than freedom or truth.

Cults in America: Programmed for Paradise. Appel, Willa. 1985. New York: Henry Holt.

An interesting nonfiction book that discusses the mentality and working of cults, cult leaders, and members from an historical perspective. Most applicable to this theme-set is the material on how leaders structure cults to attract and retain followers who will respond with loyalty to leaders who have provided them with what they perceive as their own personal utopia.

Looking Backward: 2000–1887. Bellamy, Edward. 2003. New York: Broadview.

Originally published in 1888, *Looking Backward* has been described as one of the most influential utopian novels in English. Julian West goes to sleep in 1887 and wakes up in 2000. The competitive capitalism of late nineteenth-century America has been replaced by a cooperative society in which every worker receives the same wage.

Utopia. More, Thomas. 1997. New York: Dover.

Sir Thomas More, a sixteenth-century scholar, envisions an island paradise where people practice religious tolerance, share all goods communally as well as a common work ethic, and have forsaken violence and corruption. This edition also includes "The Sileni of Alcibiades" as well as a helpful introduction and notes.

USING THE UTOPIAN/DYSTOPIAN THEME-SET

Because we have chosen *Fahrenheit 451* as the core text of this set, some specific themes develop that more narrowly focus the set of books identified in our annotated theme-set. We will begin with the broadest concept, the chapter title itself.

Utopianism

Utopianism has been defined as "the dreams and nightmares that concern the ways in which groups of people arrange their lives and that usually envision a radically different society than the one in which the dreamers live" (Lyman Tower Sargent qtd. in Hintz and Ostry 2003, 2). Fantasy often plays a significant role in the story, even though the changes may not be radical at all, and the social system could be more simplistic than that demonstrated in *Fahrenheit 451*. The defining element is that the ideal toward which the characters aspire is social in nature. *Weslandia, Roxaboxen*, and the imaginary world of the wild things in the Maurice Sendak classic, *Where the Wild Things Are*, are all examples of safe places for children where they believe their idea of justice will prevail. In *Weslandia*, Wesley begins with a development that is essentially a natural environment in which he must sustain himself, but his social circumstances change when the children who tease him in school want to be involved, and he becomes the "king of the realm," admired, rather than tormented.

Many utopian books are set in the world of the author but contain a secondary fantasy world that may be visited as is the case in *Peter Pan*, *The Secret Garden*, and of course, the *Harry Potter* series. The authors adeptly compare the circumstances of the two worlds that may or may not be free of attack from evil. Part of the utopian genre for children and young adults is the significant role they play in protecting their idealized world from negative influences that may threaten it. As is the case with most pictures of perfection, flaws insidiously creep into the scene: Peter cannot have Wendy and never grow up; Harry Potter and his friends battle the forces of evil; Max finds that it's not so great to be king if no one loves him.

Most dystopian books are set some time in the future. Futuristic societies should profit from our knowledge about how to make a society better and the readily available use of technology to improve our day-to-day existence, but our human tendency to take things to the extreme seems to prevail in literature as it probably will in real life (*No Kidding*), and the pesky seven deadly sins rear their heads, threatening to destroy any potentially ideal world. Books such as *The Giver* and *Off the Road* also demonstrate a human propensity to eliminate the imperfect even if the imperfect is human. Old age is as abhorrent as ever (so much for changing human attitudes through a wave of aging baby boomers), and heaven help the baby who does not meet society's demand for fitting in. As technologically advanced as the worlds are in many dystopian novels, human behavior reverts to the primitive. Remember the ancient Greeks who left imperfect babies out on the hillsides for the wolves to find (or a kindly shepherd whose sensibilities were not as finely honed)? Lois Lowry sets two of her dystopian novels, *Gathering Blue* and *Messenger*, in villages that are quite primitive by modern standards. It is not the technology that leads their societies to their cruel and totalitarian behaviors but rather man's inability to control the most detestable of human traits such as greed and envy.

In *Cults in America: Programmed for Paradise*, Willa Appel examines the attraction of cults for modern-day humans. What elements of a society would people value enough to abandon their current existence and come to live with a self-appointed leader? Other texts also give fictitious characters the chance to create a world from scratch (*Ice, Invitation to the Game, Brave New World*). A task such as this forces the new world inhabitants to make decisions about social organization, governance, the role of the individual, and what kinds of freedoms those who live there will have. These determinations result from the act of questioning the society from which they came. Reading utopian literature is in itself an act of questioning. What do we value, and what would we change? If change is possible, there is hope. When interviewed by Hintz and Ostry (2003), Lois Lowry was asked if young people and children can handle pure dystopia. She responded, "Young people handle dystopia every day: in their lives, their dysfunctional families, their violence-ridden schools. They watch dystopian television and movies about the real world where firearms bring about explosive conclusions to conflict. Yes, I think they need to see some hope for such a world. I can't imagine writing a book that doesn't have a hopeful ending" (xi).

Fahrenheit 451 has a hopeful ending. In fact, because of the destruction of the world by war, the Book People have the chance to start all over again with those few who remain to rebuild society and, hopefully, to demonstrate a new set of values and spirit of cooperation. They carry with them the memorized wisdom of the ages and a clear memory of what it means to live in fear on the fringes of society. The question is, Will they be able to use the best of our human nature to create a world of inclusion that values the lessons of the past?

Knowledge Versus Ignorance

A significant theme in many books in our set is the struggle between knowledge and ignorance. When characters seek to maintain a firm hand over a society, keeping their subjects in ignorance is key to their total control. This does not require a stretch of the imagination for any reader with some knowledge of history. African slaves were not taught to read nor were their descendants provided with a quality education equal to whites until the law mandated it. How many axioms proclaim the advantages of knowledge? "A little knowledge goes a long way." "Knowledge is power." Richard Wright's story as told in *Richard Wright and the Library Card* demonstrates the struggle blacks in the South experienced in trying to achieve equal access to the books that bring knowledge.

If people can be imprisoned by ignorance, governance is simplified. The more knowledge a person has, the more he or she asks questions. People who question are a danger to the balance of society. We see this fear in, *The Giver, Ice, 1984,* and *Animal Farm. Fahrenheit 451* is wholly based on the fear of the information in books and the questions it might generate. This leads us to the next suggested theme.

Censorship

Although *Fahrenheit 451* does not give us the reason for the censorship of books in its society, we can see that people have become indifferent toward books and have lost interest in reading, an issue that should be particularly frightening to us today. The loss of interest appears to be because competing forms of entertainment such as television and radio have taken the place of books. The ability to concentrate has been usurped by overstimulation caused by fast cars, clever advertisements, and loud music. Bradbury also alludes to the trend of reading condensed books, a practice brought on by the overwhelming quantity of printed material. The premise of *Fahrenheit 451* could easily exist in today's world. The hostility in the novel toward books stems from objections of special interest groups who may be offended by what the books contain. If we explore the theme of censorship thoroughly in relation to Bradbury's book, we will need to look closely at the First Amendment, both from the standpoint of being told what information we may access and the political correctness of that information.

Several books in the theme-set also address the issue of censorship. *The Rebellious Alphabet* and *Aunt Chip and the Great Triple Creek Dam Affair* show that authors believe even children should be sensitive to what happens when books, and consequently knowledge, are forbidden. *Maudie and Me and the Dirty Book* and *The Day They Came to Arrest the Book* show a slightly more sophisticated view of censorship from the standpoint of older children and young adults.

Symbolism in *Fahrenheit 451*

The theme-sets in our book have been compiled to build a thematic approach to the teaching of the core text, but in the case of *Fahrenheit 451*, we also want to mention the uses of symbolism in the text. The prevalence of such symbols as blood, mirrors, and Bradbury's specifically identified hearth and salamander and sieve and sand, would present opportunities for some intellectually provocative discussions. They also lend themselves to interpretation through multiple-intelligences activities, especially using visual and spatial representations.

ACTIVITIES USING MULTIPLE INTELLIGENCES

The Founding Fathers established the Bill of Rights after having experienced tyranny and repression in the lands of their birth. The official control of information in their homelands left them with no right to govern their own education, and when they began their lives in their new world, they determined they would have all the freedoms they lacked in their old worlds. Thus was born the First Amendment to the Constitution.

Activity 1: Poster of Similarities and Differences

The First Amendment to the Constitution is the basis for decisions regarding the rights of individuals to express their diverse beliefs, whether religious, political, or educational: "Congress shall make no law respecting an establishment of religion, or prohibiting the free exercise thereof; or abridging the freedom of speech, or of the press; or the right of the people peaceably to assemble, and to petition the government for a redress of grievances."

In *Fahrenheit 451*, Guy Montag lives in an alternate world from the one in which U.S. citizens live today. Or does he? Divide the students into literacy circles of four or five. They are to construct a poster comparing the rules of Montag's society in the novel with the rules and habits of current society in the United States. This poster must have at least six elements for each society and must have examples of each element as it exists within the novel and within society today. Somewhere on the poster, the group must give two statements of belief, one for each society, in which the elements are incorporated. Hang the posters around the room for a gallery walk at a specified time. This will precede the next activity. (Spatial, Interpersonal)

Activity 2: Let's Discuss . . .

Using the posters as the source for material, conduct an inner–outer circle discussion in which the entire class participates. Divide the class into two groups. Arrange seating for everyone so that there is an inner circle of chairs surrounded by an outer circle of chairs. Ask each group to respond in writing to the following statement: *How is it possible to protect citizens without taking away rights?*

As the teacher, you will need to give students an example for the above question. This might be something from current news, or it could be a personal experience or a situation you've heard about. When you are finished, seat one group in the inner circle, and leave one chair open. The students in the inner circle are to discuss their responses to the above statement while members of the outer circle merely listen, watch, and take notes. If there is a time when someone from the outer circle wishes to join the inner circle briefly to make a comment, that person may take the empty seat in the inner circle long enough to make the response but must leave the inner circle when the response is finished. Sometime within the discussion period, you will need to have the circles change places so that the inner circle of people then become the listeners, observers, and the note-takers. At the end of the discussion time, ask all students to make a "once around the table" oral statement to conclude the discussion. No one may interrupt or continue the discussion after this point. The notes taken during the discussion are valuable texts themselves when debriefing the activity. Students who take notes on what others say will refer to those notes when they write a reflective statement at the end of the activity. Such inquiry-based work lays the foundation for essay, discussion, and further research.

Students enjoy discussing such meaty issues. They can readily identify with the loss of freedoms involving issues of public safety such as when they subject their belongings (and bodies) to search before boarding an airplane, or in another example, when workers or athletes must submit to periodic drug testing. Even if students are not old enough to remember how it "used to be" before terrorists attacks occurred on U.S. soil, they know from history lessons that some safeguards in place today have contributed to peoples' freedom from fear while others may go too far in infringing upon individual rights. Reading and discussing such issues brings new understanding of vital issues such as the freedoms Americans enjoy. (Interpersonal, Linguistic)

Activity 3: The Mountain Lions Versus Public Safety

In a perfect world, animals and humans would be able to coexist in the same habitat. As of this publication, though, the Arizona Fish and Game Department is embroiled in a battle to protect citizens in areas where mountain lions used to be free to roam without interference. Tucson has grown around the habitat where many lions still roam, and because of the proximity, the lions have become accustomed to being near people. Mountain lions have been seen near schools in the daytime; some have even threatened humans. Because many in the public desire to preserve the lives of the mountain lions even if they threaten people, the Fish and Game Department is attempting to control these wild animals' potential attacks on people by having the lions removed for relocation in wild game parks. In addition, the State Department of Agriculture has a list of noxious weeds and trees that threaten agriculture and food production. What would a perfect society look like if all traces of these natural "elements" were removed? Ask students to research the issues of wild animals or noxious weeds and other plants in their environment. After researching, ask them to create a "pro" or "con" statement listing the advantages or disadvantages of this removal. They will need to list collateral effects as well, such as the loss of jobs and the elimination of special interest groups currently concerned with such issues. When they are finished, they will need to come to a conclusion as to the best course of action in preserving the environment and peoples' lives. The final product could be a persuasive essay in which they explore the issue.

Because writing persuasively is a learned skill, students need to approach such an assignment by building background knowledge first. Any cogently written argument must have the strength of knowledge and awareness as its basis. Most students attempting this kind of writing do not have innate knowledge, so they must acquire it before they can write well. Informational texts help add this background, and hearing others' viewpoints in order to see issues from different viewpoints will crystallize the necessary information. (Linguistic, Environmental)

Activity 4: Political Cartoon

Students will design a political cartoon that depicts a utopian/dystopian society as it appears in a novel within the theme-set. They will then explain their cartoon to the class. Adding a visual element to any discussion based upon the texts encourages students to reform their thinking and to see issues from different viewpoints. (Spatial, Linguistic)

Activity 5: Absolute Power Corrupts Absolutely

Using the preceding statement ("absolute power corrupts absolutely"), ask the students individually to list current world issues in which the statement is true. Then, direct them to combine their lists with those of their theme-set reading group and then to categorize the list into sections for which their literacy circle group decides the labels. On one paper, they are to list events within the text that would also illustrate the issues their group has raised. At this point, the teacher needs to discuss with them what conclusions can be drawn about power and the use of power. Issues that are collaboratively discussed tend to create common understandings upon which text meaning can be built. Using shared interpretations can connect students to issues to which they would normally give only surface attention, and it builds a deeper understanding of themes and world issues, thus allowing students to address other similar issues with new insight. (Linguistic, Intrapersonal, Interpersonal, Logical-Mathematical)

Activity 6: Inductive Writing

Most school writing asks students to write a topic sentence followed by general statements supporting that topic sentence. Instead, ask students to try inductive writing. For this kind of writing, students begin with the anecdote and build to the conclusive sentence, which in this case will be one of the following quotes. Figure 7–1 models a brief inductive paragraph using a famous quote as the concluding sentence. For this exercise, give the students the following five statements from *Fahrenheit 451*:

1. We need to be really bothered once in a while.
2. Don't think. Thinking is the enemy of creativity.
3. I'm seventeen and I'm crazy. My uncle says the two always go together.

I've always thought that I couldn't write very well until the day that my teacher assigned me the task of writing an article about my best friend, a victim of a huge Tsunami in Indonesia. My best friend and her family were in Indonesia visiting relatives at the time, and they never came home. We found out later that my friend and her family had been washed out to sea. All my thoughts were with them, and I felt deep sadness for the way her young life and those of her family had been taken away. We had been best friends since we were four. Her house next door was just the way it always had been, but the family was never coming home. This horrible tragedy affected me deeply. Now here I was with the task of writing about her. At first, I struggled and worried that I couldn't do a good job because I felt so strongly. But then, I thought of all the terrific fun we had as friends. It would be a shame if I couldn't remember those times later, so I started to write about our times together. The words started to flow and it became easy to write about someone I loved so much. My teacher read my paper overnight, and the next day, he told me that it was quite moving. Then he told me something I remember to this day. He said that I just needed to understand that writing was a way of loosening creative feelings. He said, **"Don't think. Thinking is the enemy of creativity."**

FIGURE 7–1 *A Brief Inductive Paragraph Using a Quote as the Conclusion*

4. You've got to jump off cliffs all the time and build your wings on the way down.
5. Those who don't build, must burn.

Then ask the students to create a paragraph of their own using one of these five quotes as their concluding sentence. Ask them to share their creations. This kind of writing is one way to increase students' ability to manipulate sentences and create meaning by varying their style. Depending upon the type of quotes you offer for them to use, this exercise can also be quite enjoyable. (Linguistic, Logical-Mathematical)

Activity 7: Censorship

Simplistically, *Fahrenheit 451* is a book about choice. In this country, because we have so many Constitutionally based freedoms, we have become accustomed to exercising our rights, including the right to choose books we wish to read, but the clash between those who wish to protect society against undesirable printed influences and those who wish to interpret the First Amendment liberally makes for frequent headline news. Ask students to go to the banned books website maintained by American Library Association (www.ala.org). They are to find the most challenged book list at this site and to look only at the titles of the books listed. Using *only* the titles listed, students are to make a list of the six most popular reasons why books might be challenged. In literacy circles of four to six, students are then to select one of the reasons for which they as a group are to "play the devil's advocate." After carefully considering their selected "reason," they are to create a statement of purpose (rationale) for the group advocating banning books based upon their "reason." For example, if one of the reasons happened to be "Books about dragons cause small children to be fearful," then their public statement would be the rationale for banning such books. After all statements are created, collect and redistribute the rationales to the literacy circle groups, making sure that no group has its own statement. The assignment then is for the groups to write a reasoned response to refute the statement. Post all statements and responses for at least a day so that all may read the statements and responses. Then, conduct a discussion focusing on the questions:

- Why is book banning such an emotional issue?
- What books have they read that should be banned (or not)?
- Overall, what would they consider to be a convincing argument for banning any book?

This assignment could result in writing a persuasive essay, or it could simply serve as a means for increasing interest in one of the novels. The technique of arguing from an opposite viewpoint from their true stance allows students to become better writers. Through practice, if they develop the ability to anticipate the questions or the argument against their views, they have a greater means to make logical and more meaningful connections for the readers of their essays. (Interpersonal, Linguistic)

The situations present in this theme-set as well as the activities are relevant to all of our lives today. Students have more background knowledge and opinions about the themes of a perfect world and censorship than they do about most topics with which they could be presented in class. A unit that requires critical thinking and persuasive skills such as this may be extended into many other realms for discussion. As a precursor to writing a research paper, utopian/dystopian literature could be the catalyst needed to develop interest in more powerful persuasive writing.

8 | SCAFFOLDING AND DEVELOPING PRIOR KNOWLEDGE

Instruction for English Learners

For students who are at the beginning stages of English, English as a second language classes are important to their linguistic growth because the teachers simplify and clarify the language for them. However, for students with an intermediate or advanced level of English proficiency, simplification will no longer suffice because at those levels students need to enhance their knowledge of more sophisticated language. In fact, simplified language is detrimental to their future development of English. Engaging students who are at the intermediate level of English proficiency in classroom environments where the emphasis is on acquiring the terms and knowledge of each of the disciplines is the key to their language growth and ultimately to their academic success (Chamot and O'Malley 1994; Cummins 1981; Scarcella 2003; Valdés 2001; Walqui 2000).

What is academic English, and how can it be acquired? Academic English is the variety of the language that is "used in professional books and characterized by the specific linguistic features associated with academic disciplines" (Scarcella 2003, 9). In other words, each academic discipline, such as English, science, mathematics, or history, has a set of words, key ideas, and discourse features that have parameters for communicating oral and written information among its members, whether in an academic setting, in private industry, or in governmental agencies. Although the definition and the specifics of academic English are relatively recent, more research is emerging on it.

The framework of academic English put forth by Scarcella (2003) includes three components: linguistic, cognitive, and sociocultural/psychological. The linguistic component includes five dimensions of language: (1) *phonology*, or sounds and letters; (2) *lexicon*, or words and their meaning; (3) *grammar*, or sentence structure; (4) *function*, or the many uses of language, such as apologizing, hypothesizing, debating, asking, explaining, and so on; and (5) *discourse*, or the genres or forms of language, such as a telephone conversation, a joke, a business letter, a memorandum, or a compare-and-contrast essay.

The cognitive component of academic English includes knowledge acquisition, higher-order thinking skills, problem-solving strategies, and metalinguistic awareness. The last of these is the knowledge needed to make reference to language itself. Common examples of metalinguistic awareness include using a dictionary, thesaurus, or style manual to make decisions about word usage or writing conventions.

The sociological/psychological component of academic English includes the advantages and benefits that accrue to people in academia, business, and government who can speak, write, and read English at this level.

Acquiring academic English skills becomes important for English learners to succeed in school. This means not assuming that English learners who seem fluent orally arrive with the basic academic English skills that many of their native-speaking counterparts have acquired. Thus, high school teachers must be willing to fold the three components of academic English (i.e., linguistic, cognitive, and the sociological/psychological components) into their subject matter instruction.

A MODEL FOR TEACHING ACADEMIC ENGLISH TO ENGLISH LEARNERS

Researchers recommend that these students learn language skills simultaneously with curricular content (Chamot and O'Malley 1994; Cummins 1981; Scarcella 2003; Walqui 1993, 2000). One model for doing this, developed by Walqui, is for secondary teachers to plan a lesson sequence and develop scaffolded tasks for students within that sequence. (For a more thorough discussion see Walqui 2003.)

Designing a Lesson Sequence

Lesson design involves three steps: (1) preparing the students; (2) having them delve into texts; and (3) extending their understanding (Walqui 1993, 2003). The teacher can prepare students for reading a book, such as Steinbeck's *The Grapes of Wrath*, in a number of ways, for example: (1) using the theme-sets to activate students' prior knowledge or to build needed background knowledge, (2) introducing new vocabulary and idiomatic phrases, (3) contextualizing the Great Depression, and (4) discussing how Steinbeck's book is written.

Activating students' prior knowledge can be accomplished specifically or broadly by tying into the book's themes. For example, to encourage students to think about migration, the teacher might ask them to recall times in their own lives when they and their families have moved to follow seasonal work or more broadly how many have moved anywhere and for whatever reason (Walqui 1993, 2003). Activating students' prior knowledge more broadly will include many more students. However, if a teacher has many if not all students whose parents are migrant farmworkers then the specific is a better teaching strategy. Finally, the teacher can build background knowledge about migrant workers during the Great Depression by showing the students photographs and art.

All teachers have their students delve into texts, whether they are teaching literature, science, or social studies. However, many English learners must additionally be taught comprehension strategies good readers use, such as summarizing material, asking relevant questions, making predictions, and clarifying information. To help students extend their understanding, teachers might have students work on an assignment that requires them to reread certain sections of a text. For example, teachers might ask their students to create a poster for the story, write a dialogue that is not in the story but might be, or write a compare-and-contrast essay (Walqui 1993, 2003).

Although some individual lessons may be helpful in promoting language growth, a sequence of tasks is preferable for promoting the sophisticated academic language that English learners will need to succeed in mainstream content classes. Thus, all three steps assist English learners to become better readers and writers through the preparation completed ahead of time and afterward in the opportunities to revisit texts with specific purposes.

Developing Specific Tasks for Students

The second component of the framework incorporates one or more of the six elements of instructional scaffolding that guide teachers to devise tasks to give their English learners access to the core curricula. These six instructional scaffolds include: (1) modeling; (2) bridging; (3) schema building; (4) contextualization; (5) metacognitive development; and (6) text representation (Walqui 1993, 2003).

Modeling provides examples of what is to be learned. For example, the teacher might list the parts of an essay that students should include or show a sample of one. Modeling is one of the key means for students to learn a new skill or concept.

Bridging connects students' personal knowledge with what is to be learned. For example, to prepare students to read John Steinbeck's *The Grapes of Wrath*, the teacher might have the students write a paragraph about a time in their lives when they might have had to move or change schools (Walqui 1993, 2003). Bridging is a scaffold that provides the motivation and stimulus for students to invest in the topic.

Schema building develops a network of concepts to explore a subject in depth. For example, the teacher might discuss a novel by using a graphic organizer with the literary elements of plot, characterization, themes, language, and setting. Schema building is important because it provides the students with the larger picture of where ideas fit and how they are connected and, in this case, from which to connect literary analysis concepts.

Contextualization creates a sensory environment to enhance learning. For example, in teaching *The Grapes of Wrath*, the teacher might show the students photographs from the Great Depression and discuss what students see about life during this time period. Again this motivates students and provides additional information that a text might not present on its own. Moreover, it provides the frame of mind for reading the novel.

Metacognitive development focuses on the student deciding on which specific strategies will be the most effective for reading with full comprehension, writing well given the purpose and genre, and choosing strategies for learning new material. For example, in order to help students make these decisions, the teacher shows students how to anticipate story lines, how to summarize sections of a text, or how to find the topic sentence of a paragraph. These are the skills that help students acquire more knowledge and become more adept at academics. The goal is for them to internalize these strategies so that students become better students at reading and writing in each of the content areas.

Text representation transforms a text into another format. For example, the teacher might ask the students to interpret a poem by drawing a picture. This provides the opportunity for the students to engage in the text more deeply because now the ideas have to been applied in a different genre.

Figure 8–1 illustrates both components of the model: lesson sequence design and the scaffolded instructional tasks. The middle column illustrates the language students are likely to encounter that is crucial to their building content and knowledge of academic English. In preparing the learner, the teacher may ask students to share their own personal experiences about a topic and thus students have opportunities for using the language. The teacher may also provide a language experience about the topic, thus modeling use of the academic language. In delving and interacting with the text, the students, again, are receiving input through the reading in which they are engaged. Finally, in the third component, extending understanding, students have opportunities to take the academic input and use it to complete the given task, thus furthering academic language.

In both parts of the model, the goal is for the content and the tasks to remain challenging (Bruner 1983). This means that the teacher does not water down the substantive curriculum, as often happens, but assists the students to accomplish difficult tasks. On the other hand, the teacher also does not overwhelm the students with content, expecting them to either sink or swim.

Lesson Design	Language and Content Developments	Scaffolded Tasks
Preparing the learner	Language input/ language output	Scaffolded task 1 Scaffolded task 2
Delving and interacting with the text	Language input and negotiation of language input	Scaffolded task 3 Expected task: Reading the text Expected task: Discussing the text
Extending understanding	Output and negotiation of input	Scaffolded task 4 Expected task: written assignment (essay)

FIGURE 8–1 *Lesson Design and Scaffolded Tasks Models*

In the example in Figure 8–2, the teacher expects the students to read the text, discuss it, and write an essay about it. Thus, the expectation about writing a composition based on a literature selection is still present. However, there are several prereading tasks that can help English learners with threshold levels of English to accomplish an assignment like an essay. When teachers assign English learners to read texts, both fiction and nonfiction, the teachers should first prepare the students by selecting any appropriate tasks such as pointing out personal connections between the students' knowledge and the material (bridging), bringing in a photograph (contextualizing), watching a silent two-minute video clip of a scene from the story (again contextualizing), and so on. If the teachers were simply to assign the texts without this preparation, the students would probably have more difficulty comprehending the material or may not be motivated to read the text. Figure 8–2 provides an example of a sequence of tasks and the instructional scaffolds needed to have English learners successfully complete reading a novel, for example.

Figure 8–2 illustrates the orchestration of the two frameworks. The teacher plans, say, two tasks that prepare the students (tasks 1 and 2 in column 3); one task that helps the students to practice an important reading skill (task 3 in column 3); and one task that gives the students the opportunity to practice using language, in this case academic language (task 4 in column 3). The tasks that the teacher chooses to prepare the students are ones that tap into the students' personal knowledge. This is key because it motivates and directs the students' attention to the theme of the core novel. Motivated and focused students can now begin to engage with the text in meaningful ways.

The two tasks that we have chosen to illustrate the process of preparing students are pedagogical examples of the elements of scaffolding—bridging and contextualization. For bridging students' personal knowledge with the theme of the core literature book, the teacher could choose to have a quickwrite, or a quick sketch, or a think-pair-share activity. To further prepare the students, the teacher can choose to show a picture, show a silent two-minute video clip, or play music. This element of scaffolding (contextualization) helps the English learners visualize while the teacher introduces new vocabulary and uses academic language.

Now the teacher is ready to present the core of the lesson—reading a specific chapter or section. English learners at the intermediate or early advanced levels of oral proficiency may not be able to read the text with sufficient comprehension. Thus, the teacher must couple reading the text with an introduction of reading skills that good readers use (Palinscar and Brown 1984). At that point, the teacher can introduce any specific comprehension skill—for example, any of the four comprehension skills of reciprocal teaching: asking good questions, summarizing, predicting, and clarifying. It is recommended that the teacher not have English learners practice all four skills at once, but rather one at a time, on four separate occasions. In that way, students can learn each of the skills thoroughly and have time to assimilate each (Walqui 1993). Once they have practiced all four individually they can orchestrate all four

Lesson Design	Language and Content Development	Task	Instructional Scaffold Used
Preparing the learner	Opportunities for input *and* output	Task 1: Read and view text sets	Task 1: Contextualization
		Task 2: Quickwrite	Task 2: Bridging
Delving and interacting with the text	Opportunities for input	Task 3: Practice one reading comprehension strategy at a time (e.g., summarizing) with text	Task 3: Metacognitive development
		Expected task: Read the text with the reading strategy taught	Task 4: Metacognitive development
	Opportunities for negotiation of input	Expected task: Discuss the text	Expect task—discussion: schema building
Extending understanding	Opportunities for output *and* negotiation of input	Task 5: Compare-and-contrast chart of two books (e.g., with one previously read)	Task 5: Schema building and meta-cognitive development
		Task 6: Compare-and-contrast essay or collaborative poster	Task 6: Text-representation

FIGURE 8–2 *Integrating the Lesson Design Sequence and the Elements of Instructional Scaffolding*

skills. Also, the students should not read the entire chapter using the reading skill, but should practice, say, the first six or eight paragraphs.

To practice the comprehension skill, the teacher can have the students practice with partners. The first partner can read aloud and ask one good question that the second partner will answer (Walqui 2003). The teacher can then discuss the students' questions and answers. After that, the students can read the text silently on their own, or the teacher can read aloud while the students follow along silently. In a grand conversation, the teacher and students can respond to the story and discuss its literary elements. By both practicing one reading skill and responding to literary qualities, the English learners will be more likely to understand most of the story.

In the last sequence of tasks, extending understanding, the teacher provides an opportunity for the English learners to use the academic language that the teacher introduced and that was encountered in the novel. This is the key to English learners acquiring the academic English that they will need to succeed in the mainstream English curriculum. The tasks that the teacher can choose for extending understanding include having the students construct a collaborative poster, write a collaborative dialogue, or write a compare-and-contrast essay (Walqui 2003). In the collaborative poster, for example, the teacher can invite the students to draw a critical detail or an important scene from the novel, select two quotes that are important to the story, and choose an original phrase that represents details from the story (Walqui 2003). The teacher may use any other literary elements that seem appropriate, such as character description, but should keep them simple the first time around. For the compare-and-contrast essay, a much more difficult task for English learners, it is important that the teacher help the students organize that essay using a compare-and-contrast chart. The students can write the essay more effectively from the information from the chart (Walqui 2003). Modeling sentences that illustrates how to contrast or how to compare are crucial for many English learners as they write in this new genre.

Because the poster requires collaboration, the teacher must ensure that all members of the group be responsible for contributing. This can be done by asking each member to use a different-color marker and noting this somewhere on a legend on the poster (Walqui 2003). Because the teacher has asked the students to choose two quotes and come up with an original phrase, they will think about, discuss, and reread sections of the novel. This is what extends understanding and allows for deeper comprehension. Moreover, as the teacher structures the tasks to extend understanding, the students begin to expand their repertoire of the English language and the mainstream literature curricular content.

PRIOR KNOWLEDGE AND COMPREHENSION

Using prior knowledge to understand the text is one strategy that good readers use. In its simplest definition prior knowledge is the information that develops from previous experiences. In the literature on reading comprehension it is also the cognitive structures or the network of concepts stored in memory that are abstract representations of events, objects, and relationships (Anderson and Pearson 1984). Everyone possesses prior knowledge and good readers activate it to help them understand what they are reading. An individual's cognitive structures are organized so that the individual can recall general and specific features of a concept. Individuals possess both general and specific features about concepts. For example, in the concept of condors the mind is organized so that the individual accesses the general characteristics about "birds" (for example, they have wings, feathers, lay eggs) and then specific characteristics that distinguish condors from most other types of birds (for example, they are vultures with a large wing span, the California condor became extinct but biologists have experimented with breeding and caring for the young as a way to increase their numbers). As individuals acquire life experiences, prior knowledge is built. Teachers and scholars know that prior knowledge can also be built through extensive reading about experiences that they will never have, for example, learning about penguins.

Prior knowledge is a highly recommended strategy to enhance comprehension because it helps readers comprehend the text more quickly (Pressley 2002; Zimmerman and Keene 1997). All readers bring to the reading their knowledge that is built up through their life experiences; however, being able to access it readily when reading makes a difference in better comprehension. Prior knowledge has been found to be a strategy that can be taught to students in order to improve their understanding of the text (Anderson and Pearson 1984; Levin and Pressley 1981; Pressley 2002). Prior knowledge is identified as an important strategy that teachers should teach and make readers aware of. It is to help bridge the new information, say from the text, with the older knowledge.

Having a rich store of prior knowledge on a topic allows for faster access in reading a text. The fast access frees the mind's attention resources for other dimensions of comprehension such as critically evaluating the ideas expressed in a text. Having students create a semantic map of a topic is an excellent way to determine the strength of a student's prior knowledge. Students who include branches and categories in their semantic maps suggest a richness and strength in their knowledge base. Conversely, students may have limited prior knowledge and may have misconceptions about the topic, in which case, reading, discussing, and if possible direct experiences are key to countering those misconceptions.

Teachers know that having students make connections to their own lives (text-to-self connections), other texts (text-to-text), and to the world (text-to-world) improves comprehension. Furthermore, helping students make connections with other texts is a mark of a literate person. Thus teachers who use the semantic maps, KWL charts (stating what they know about the subject, what they would like to know, and finally, what they've learned about the subject) (Fisher and Frey 2004), anticipatory guides, quickwrites, quick sketches, and pictures to help students make connections during the literature discussions are tapping into this powerful comprehension strategy.

However, prior knowledge can interfere with new knowledge that is presented. Prior knowledge is part of the monitoring strategies that readers use to comprehend the text. Prior knowledge affects comprehension of a text. The more prior knowledge a student has about a topic, the better the comprehension. Students have to learn that the connections they can make to their own lives (text-to-self connections), other texts (text-to-text), and to the world (text-to-world) improve comprehension. Motivation and confidence also come, not just comprehension, when students make those connections. Good readers use their background knowledge to monitor their understanding of the story (Pressley 2002).

With the large number of English learners in schools today, multicultural readings are important to increase English learners' comprehension of text. Because picture books use both art and text to convey a theme or concept, for students who have not had previous U.S. curricular experiences, picture books and early young adult books provide a bridge to the high school core novel, essay, or play. In addition, the picture books chosen are meant for English learners and other nonmainstream students, giving them opportunities to see themselves reflected in the themes of the core literature.

Moreover, not all students in U.S. high schools are from mainstream homes—that is, a large number of students reside in ethnic households. For these students, their experiences of growing up ethnic in America are not discussed. Thus, for these students, a growing up ethnic theme would help them better relate to the classics.

9 | THE CHANGING FACE OF PUBLIC SCHOOL STUDENTS

ENGLISH LEARNERS

Nearly anyone who has been involved in U.S. public schools over the last decade cannot help but notice that our student population has been experiencing a demographic change. Between 1990 and 2000, there was a 46 percent increase in the number of English learners[1] in the United States, from 2.3 million to 3.4 million. In comparison, the school population between the ages of five and seventeen increased by only 17 percent, from 45 million to 53 million (U.S. Department of Education). During the 2000–2001 academic year over 44 percent of all English learners were concentrated in pre–K through grade 3, 35 percent were in the middle grades, 19 percent were enrolled in high schools, and 2 percent were in ungraded classrooms (Kindler 2002). Although they enter at all grade levels, the majority of English learners do so at the early elementary grades (K–2) and in ninth grade (Kindler 2002).

The six states that have the greatest number of English learners in the grades between pre–K and 12 are: California (1.5 million), Texas (570,000), Florida (255,000), New York (240,000), Illinois (140,500), and Arizona (135,000). Fifteen states (Alabama, Arkansas, Georgia, Idaho, Indiana, Iowa, Kansas, Kentucky, Minnesota, Nebraska, Nevada, North Carolina, Oregon, South Carolina, and Tennessee) have collectively doubled the number of English learners since 1990 (Kindler 2002).

English learners come from all parts of the world, but 80 percent are from Spanish-speaking countries and regions (Kindler 2002). Forty-two states listed Spanish as the language spoken by the majority of their English learners; eight states reported another language other than Spanish: Alaska (Yup'ik), Hawaii (Ilocano), Maine (French), Minnesota (Hmong), Montana (Blackfoot), North Dakota (various Native American languages), South Carolina (Lakota), and Vermont (Serbo-Croatian). The next largest language group speaks various

---

1 The term *English learners* is used because it denotes a positive perspective of students who are learning English; however, the federal government officially uses the term *limited-English proficient*.

Asian languages: Vietnamese, 2 percent; Hmong, 1.5 percent; Cantonese Chinese, 1.2 percent; and Korean, 1 percent (Kindler 2002).

English learners usually arrive with no English language proficiency but with varying competence with respect to subject matter. Cristina, Luis, and Martin (pseudonyms) represent three typical English learners.

Cristina

Cristina came to the United States with her parents from Mexico at the age of six and entered first grade at Jefferson Elementary School with no command of English whatsoever. She was placed in regular mainstream classrooms and was pulled out for forty-five minutes of English as a second language (ESL) instruction. Eventually she learned to communicate in English; however, her reading and writing lagged behind her oral skills. When she graduated from Jefferson, she was placed in an ESL-4 class at Washington Middle School because she did not have the necessary command of English to be assigned to a regular English class. Now in seventh grade, her reading and writing skills are at the fourth-grade level. She is taking general math, general science, physical education, and an elective technology class in the regular school program. Although Cristina can communicate orally with her teachers fairly well one-on-one, in class she is soft-spoken and shy. She rarely raises her hand to answer any of her teachers' questions because she feels that her classmates can communicate much better than she can.

Luis

Luis, a ninth grader at Golden Hills High School, arrived in this country with his parents three months ago from El Salvador. He has been assigned to ESL-1, but he is also taking a number of mainstream courses, including algebra, science, reading, and physical education. At first, he had been assigned to general math, but his teacher soon realized that the work was too easy for Luis and moved him to the algebra class. Luis does fairly well in that class on everything except word problems that require a higher level of English literacy and understanding than he presently possesses. Nevertheless, in the little time that he has been here, he has learned quite a bit of English; he can communicate his basic needs and answer relatively easy questions that peers and teachers ask of him.

Martin

Martin, a tenth grader at Springfield High School, has been in this country for three years, having come with his parents from a remote mountain village in Guatemala. Before coming here, he dropped out of school after fourth grade in order to help his parents with their farming. Soon after arriving in the United States, he entered eighth grade in Highland Middle School with no command of English. Because his schooling had been interrupted for three years in Guatemala, he has had considerable difficulty with the content classes. Now, in tenth grade, he has been placed in ESL-2, is making progress in his classes, and participates in the after-school tutoring program.

Although a large number of English learners enroll in U.S. schools for the first time in kindergarten or first grade like Cristina, there are many who enter at each of the other grades, including middle and high school like Luis and Martin. The higher the grade level at which these students enter U.S. schools, the less exposure they have to American language arts and social studies concepts. On the other hand, students like Luis arrive with a firm grounding in subject content and only have to master the English language in order to adapt to the American educational system, whereas the students like Cristina and Martin must master both the language and the content areas simultaneously. The students like Martin are at a greater disadvantage than the students like Cristina because the subject areas are much more complex in high school than in the elementary grades.

THE STUDENTS' NEEDS

Students identified as English learners have a wide range of needs that can tax even the most experienced teachers. The language proficiency of these learners varies from beginning to advanced. Proficiency can be defined as knowledge of language from an individual cognitive perspective and from a social perspective. From the individual perspective, language proficiency is (1) the spontaneous use of language and structured language knowledge, such as stock phrases; (2) the control of grammatical structures; and (3) the capacity to use language in completing cognitive tasks, such as discussing an oral story (August and Hakuta 1997). From the social perspective, language proficiency involves (1) having pragmatic communicative skills, such as knowing when and how to use formal and informal language; (2) keeping a conversation going rather than just answering the conversational partner's questions; and (3) interpreting the social meaning of the speaker's intentions (Hymes 1974; Romaine 1989).

Although a teacher may be friendly in a classroom situation, the student is still expected to use more formal language than when speaking with a buddy. As for initiating questions in conversations, less proficient second language learners often let native speakers carry the dialogue. However, few native speakers will want to carry on both sides of a conversation and will tend to cut it short, thereby reducing the opportunities for the second language learners to use their second language skills. As for interpreting the social meanings of a speaker's intentions, appropriateness and politeness of language are expected. For example, second language learners must discover that not all statements seemingly phrased as questions really *are* questions. A teacher who says, "Are you putting your book away?" might subtly be voicing a command. Thus, learning a new language with the competence of a native speaker requires time, often six to nine years, depending on the opportunities to hear and use the language repeatedly in varied contexts.

To be considered competent language users according to the standards set by Teachers of English to Speakers of Other Languages, or TESOL (2004), English learners must be able to:

1. use English to communicate in social settings
2. use academic English in all content areas
3. use English in socially and culturally appropriate ways

Acquiring all three areas of language development makes learning the second language a demanding task, which for a larger number of students can take up to five to seven years (August and Hakuta 1997).

To help teachers identify English learners' second language development, TESOL (2004) uses three levels of language proficiency—beginning, intermediate, and advanced—whereas other organizations or agencies use more. For example, the California Department of Education (2004) uses five—beginning, early intermediate, intermediate, early advanced, and advanced. Although the proficiency levels are general categories, they nonetheless help teachers identify the kind of language development English learners need. Although it may be obvious to the reader, unfortunately, English learners are referred to as one monolithic group, but the reality is that their language development needs vary greatly from one proficiency category to another.

Aside from their obvious linguistic needs, English learners must also master content to succeed in school. That requires them to build intricate and multiple networks of knowledge in mathematics, the sciences, the social sciences, and the arts and humanities, including literature. In other words, they must learn facts, ideas, skills, and strategies within each of the content areas. They are also expected to be able to explain concepts, make hypotheses, predict events, infer details, report information, and arrange sequences. The difficulty of performing all of these tasks and students' perceptions that they are not able to do them competently often lead to lowered self-esteem. A second language learner, Antti Jalava, a Finnish boy who moved with his family from Finland to Sweden, expresses his need for the academic dimension of language in the following personal story:

> At school I did worse and worse, I simply couldn't understand the textbooks, no matter how hard I tried. I began to believe that really I was unusually stupid, and when I was around fourteen, I had the first sensations of self-hatred. . . . (Jalava 1988, 162)

Although reading requires students to derive meaning from the printed words on a page, writing requires them to think spontaneously, using the general organizational structures of various literary genres. The essay genre, for example, might be organized into, say, persuasive arguments or compare-and-contrast elements.

Spelling presents a particularly difficult challenge in writing English, as English spelling has many exceptions compared to phonetic languages like Spanish. Thus, when second language writers use the phonetic systems of their native languages, the invented spelling may confuse even the most experienced teachers or lead them to underestimate the skills or imagination of the writers (Hernandez 2001). For example, Latino second language writers who are considered poor writers in English tend to misspell such common words as *them* (often spelling it *dem*), *with* (spelling it *withe* and *whit*), and *little* (often spelling it *letl* or *lito*), which first language children are expected to know by second or third grade.

Once English learners acquire sufficient English, they are reclassified to fluent English proficient. These students are the success cases. Some states continue to monitor the progress of fluent English proficient students, but many do not. Nationwide during the 2000–2001 academic year, on average, 10 percent of all English learners were reclassified, with third grade (17.9 percent) and fifth grade (17.2 percent) having the largest percentage of reclassified students. As a group, English learners do not fair well in the U.S. educational system; a large number are retained, others drop out, and still others are ESL lifers (Kindler 2002; Valdés 2001). Schools need to be more vigilant about this group of students in order to ensure success.

FACTORS THAT HELP LEARNERS RAPIDLY ACQUIRE A SECOND LANGUAGE

Today much more is known about how to help students learn in their second language than the practices English learners experienced in the past. A number of writers—Luis Rodriguez, Esmeralda Santiago, and Antti Jalava—talk about their situation in schools. The following is Luis Rodriguez's experience as a six-year-old entering school in Watts, California for the first time:

> The first day of school said a lot about my scholastic life to come. I was taken to a teacher who didn't know what to do with me. She complained about not having any room, about kids who didn't even speak the language. And how was she supposed to teach anything under these conditions. Although I didn't speak English, I understood a large part of what she was saying. I knew I wasn't wanted. . . .
>
> After some more paperwork, I was taken to another class. This time the teacher appeared nicer, but distracted. She got the word about my language problem. "Okay, why don't you sit here in the back of the class," She said. "Play with some blocks until we figure out how to get you more involved." (26)

Antti Jalava's experience is situated in a third grade in Stockholm, Sweden; nevertheless, it is pertinent within the context of the United States.

> My parents were welcome, sure enough, but as far as we kids were concerned, matters were altogether different. After all, we were not

useful, productive, and on top of everything else we couldn't even speak Swedish. The principal of my new school did not really know what to do with me when I was admitted; she escorted me to the elementary third-grade classroom. We walked hand in hand. Holding hands was the only language we had in common. (161)

Esmeralda Santiago talks about her first experiences as a student entering junior high school in New York City.

All my brothers and sisters were sent back one grade so they could all learn English, so I walked to the junior high school alone. . . . We were outcasts in a school where the smartest eighth graders were in the 8–1 homeroom; each subsequent drop in number indicating one notch less smarts. I was in 8–23. . . . My class was, in some ways, the equivalent of seventh grade, perhaps even sixth or fifth. (228, 232)

Fortunately, today, schools are much more enlightened and prepared to work with English learners. Moreover, a number of resources exist to assist teachers with this challenge (for example, Center for Applied Linguistics; the state affiliates of National Association for Bilingual Education; Gibbons 2002; TESOL; Valdés 2001; Walqui 2003).

There are several factors that influence (1) how quickly English learners master the language and (2) the sophistication of the variety of English they master, from the street to the academic variety. At a minimum, the learners need to hear and read the language, which some theorists call "input" (Cummins 1981; Krashen 1981), and to have opportunities to use the language in speech and writing, which some theorists call "output" (Long 1983; Swain 1986). Exposure to English is not sufficient and is considered an inadequate means for learning the type of English needed for success.

In order for English learners to acquire the necessary vocabulary and grammar to communicate in their new language, they need input that is comprehensible (that is, input that contains some new elements that they understand)—for example, what the speaker said through face-to-face cues and gestures (Krashen 1981). The comprehensible input must also be delivered in ways that make the learners feel safe, which will allow them to maximize the amount of information they take in. The more anxious or nervous they are in communicating in the second language, the less they will take in. Moreover, for success in school, the comprehensible input should be delivered in the academic language that is used in the content areas. Academic language is characterized by its abstract nature, cognitive demands, and lack of context clues—as, for example, in a science textbook.

As for output, it is important for second language learners to produce utterances that are comprehensible to others (Swain 1986), as well as to have opportunities to engage in extensive dialogue (Gibbons 2002). It is the interaction (hearing and responding) with other speakers that promotes language acquisition. Walqui (1993, 2003) suggests that second language learners with threshold levels of English (intermediate levels and above) be given challenging writing assignments that require interaction with others—for example, collaborating with other students on inventing dialogue for a section of a novel they are studying.

Instruction for second language learners not only needs to be comprehensible, but ideally should also be "scaffolded" (Gibbons 2002; Walqui 1993, 2003). A literal scaffold is a temporary ladder that allows painters, muralists, or construction workers to reach places that they could not reach on their own in order to complete their work in sections. Similarly, scaffolded instruction includes crafting lessons and using talk to support students as they master tasks that are initially difficult. Additionally, scaffolded instruction additionally helps English learners to access or understand the core curriculum by dividing it into comprehensible parts.

Scaffolding students' learning does not mean simplifying their tasks but rather manipulating their participation in those tasks (Bruner 1983). That is, depending on the students' language competency, they will participate peripherally, modestly, or fully. In order for students to become competent in a second language, their teachers need to hand over the responsibility of learning to them. For students with an intermediate level of English, teachers should structure tasks so that the students do not work individually but in small groups, which will give them models of native competency.

Use of group work requires teachers to be familiar with some key principles of social learning. One of the problems with group work is that some students may dominate and do most of the work while others sit back passively. Additionally, English learners at the beginning and intermediate levels of proficiency may not have the necessary range of English to fully participate. Thus, it is essential to structure tasks so that the completed task depends on all members contributing relatively equally, known as interdependent tasks. Cohen and Lotan (1997) as well as Walqui (1993, 2003) have many useful suggestions for how teachers can accomplish this objective.

Unfortunately, in many schools, nonnative speakers are often isolated from the native ones, either actively or passively. For example, the school may place all beginning language learners in ESL classes, thereby separating them from the general population (Valdés 2001). Although English learners may have acquired an intermediate level of English, many (like Cristina) may hesitate to initiate a conversation with a native speaker because they feel that their English is inadequate. This self-isolation, in turn, further inhibits language development. One way to counter at least the self-isolation of English learners is to include some assignments that require group work with interdependent tasks (see Cohen and Lotan 1997).

Our theme-set concept, which has been designed to be used in regular classrooms, gives English teachers a structure for working effectively with English learners. The core literature is introduced via picture books that assist visualization, followed by short chapter books that assist focused study on a related topic. This allows English learners to access major literary themes by reactivating their prior firsthand knowledge and expanding their background knowledge.

The discussions about each of the picture books and chapter books will also provide comprehensible input that can expand students' background knowledge, placing them in a better position to understand the core literature. Once the students are immersed in reading the core literature—for example, *The Grapes of Wrath*—the teacher can use the activities included in the theme-sets to promote the use of academic language or the output that English learners with threshold levels of English (that is, intermediate and above) need.

CONCLUSION

Throughout the process of writing this book, we have spent hundreds of hours talking with and observing both elementary and secondary teachers in the classroom. When we ask what they are teaching, most often the secondary English teachers name a text or literary genre. Actually, to be more precise, we hear, "We are doing *Romeo and Juliet.*" *Doing* suggests *covering*, which is often the feeling we get when we are pressed for time in the race through the curriculum needed to teach the standards. But what is it we actually teach? Do we offer access to the enticing concepts that stimulate interest and draw in our reluctant students?

We educate our student teachers to design curriculum by first asking the big questions. "What are the enduring understandings I want my students to have at the end of this unit?" We divide the content down into more manageable pieces and ask each day, "What is it I want my students to know, be able to do, or be like at the end of this lesson?" Then we must figure out how to measure whether that learning has taken place. This process of "backward design" (Wiggins and McTighe 2000) forces us to look at why we teach literature. It's not just about a cultural literacy where students can recognize allusions to the classics on *The Simpsons*. Most students entering our credential programs say they love English because of the big ideas in the literature. How do we get from that ideal to reading a text aloud in class every day, watching the video, answering questions at the end of each chapter or writing definitions for vocabulary words, and then writing a theme essay when we've completed the book? How do we bring our students into the big conversation?

It's easier to do what we know . . . to teach the same texts each year in the same way. It's easier to fit what we know into the standards. We know that busy teachers, who are overburdened with the amount of content they must *cover*, need help with design and implementation if they are going to change a major component of their teaching. Our purpose in writing this book was to take texts you already teach and aid you with the process of scaffolding for all readers in your classes, helping them to surmount obstacles preventing their entrance into the literacy circle. We have given you some of the big ideas that bear some exploration in each theme-set, and more importantly, we have out-lined some specific tasks for your students that capitalize on multiple intelli-gences, enabling more students to successfully show you how much they know and are able to do and any attitudinal changes that have come about because of the unit of study. We incorporate student choice and collaboration with attention to meeting the needs of diverse learners. Lastly, we use sound research-based strategies that are designed to increase learning through the employment of inquiry-based activities.

It is our hope that you will be encouraged by the theoretical justification provided in Chapter 1 to move toward thematically based units that still use traditional core texts as the anchor piece and that the concrete assistance pro-vided by the logistical information in Chapter 2, the annotated bibliographies, and the theme-set activities will make the move a smooth one. What are the big ideas you want your students to gain from exploring great literature? And what kind of people do you want them to become because of their explora-tion? The best thing we can say to those outside the circle looking in is: "Come on in; the water's fine." Comfort with words builds confidence for life. Bring-ing all of our students into the literacy circle is one of the things that makes teaching English the best job in the world!

REFERENCES

ADA, ALMA FLOR. 1997. *Gathering the Sun: An Alphabet in Spanish and English.* New York: Lothrop, Lee & Shepard.

ALTMAN, LINDA JACOBS. 1993. *Amelia's Road.* New York: Lee and Low.

ANDERSON, LAURIE HALSE. 1999. *Speak.* New York: Farrar, Straus & Giroux.

ANDERSON, M. T. 2002. *Feed.* Cambridge, MA: Candlewick.

ANDERSON, RICHARD, and P. DAVID PEARSON. 1984. "A Schematic-Theoretic View of Basic Processes in Reading Comprehension." In *Handbook of Reading Research,* ed. P. David Pearson. New York: Longman.

ANGELOU, MAYA. 1969. *I Know Why the Caged Bird Sings.* New York: Random House.

ANNAN, KOFI. 2001. Acceptance speech for the Nobel Peace Prize, Oslo, Norway, December 10. Accessed 27 September 2005, www.nobel.no/eng_lect_2001b.html.

APPEL, WILLA. 1985. *Cults in America: Programmed for Paradise.* New York: Henry Holt.

ARMSTRONG, JENNIFER. 1992. *Steal Away.* New York: Orchard.

ASHABRANNER, BRENT. 1985. *Dark Harvest: Migrant Farmworkers in America.* New York: Putnam Publishing Group Library.

ATKINS, BETH. 1993. *Voices from the Fields: Children of Migrant Farmworkers Tell Their Stories.* Boston: Little, Brown.

ATWOOD, MARGARET. 1997. "Half-Hanged Mary." In *Wild Women,* ed. Melissa Mia Hall. New York: Carroll & Graf.

AUGUST, DIANE, and KENJI HAKUTA. 1997. *Improving Schooling for Language-Minority Children.* Washington, DC: National Research Council Institute of Medicine.

BALDWIN, JAMES. [1952] 1980. *Go Tell It on the Mountain.* New York: Dell.

BANKS, JAMES A., ed. 1995. *Handbook of Research on Multicultural Education.* New York: Macmillan.

BARRIE, J. M. [1911] 2000. *Peter Pan.* New York: Simon & Schuster.

BARRIO, RAYMOND. 1984. *The Plum Plum Pickers*. New York: Bilingual Review.

BATSCHE, GEORGE, and HOWARD M. KNOFF. 1994. "Bullies and Their Victims: Understanding Pervasive Problems in the Schools." *School Psychology Review* 23: 165–73.

BAUER, JOAN. 2000. *Hope Was Here*. New York: Putnam.

BAWDEN, NINA. 1998. *Off the Road*. New York: Clarion.

BEARDEN, ROMARE. 1993. *Li'l Dan, the Drummer Boy: A Civil War Story*. New York: Simon & Schuster.

BELLAMY, EDWARD. 2003. *Looking Backward: 2000–1887*. New York: Broadview.

BEMELMANS, LUDWIG. 1958. *Madeleine*. New York: Viking.

BEST, CARI. 2001. *Shrinking Violet*. New York: Farrar, Straus & Giroux.

BLAU, SHERIDAN. 2003. *The Literature Workshop: Teaching Texts and Their Readers*. Portsmouth, NH: Heinemann.

BOWKETT, STEPHEN. 2001. *Ice [The Wintering]*. London: Dolphin.

BOYD, CINDY DAWSON. 1994. *Fall Secrets*. New York: Puffin.

BRADBURY, RAY. 1967. *Fahrenheit 451*. New York: Simon & Schuster.

BRIMMER, LARRY DANE. 1992. *A Migrant Family*. Minneapolis: Lerner.

BROOKS, BRUCE. 1989. *No Kidding*. New York: Harper & Row.

BROOKS, GWENDOLYN. 1949. *Annie Allen*. Westport, CT: Greenwood.

BRUNER, JEROME. 1983. *Child's Talk*. Portsmouth, NH: Heinemann.

BRUNHOFF, JEAN DE. *Babar the King*. 1935. Translated by Merle S. Haas. New York: Random House.

BUEHL, DOUG. 2001. *Classroom Strategies for Interactive Teaching*. Newark, DE: International Reading Association.

BUNTING, EVE. 1990. *The Wall*. New York: Clarion.

———. 1994. *A Day's Work*. New York: Clarion.

———. 1996. *Going Home*. New York: HarperCollins.

———. 1998. *So Far from the Sea*. New York: Clarion.

BURNETT, FRANCES HODGSON. [1888] 1998. *The Secret Garden*. New York: HarperTrophy.

BYARS, BETSY. 1973. *The 18th Emergency*. New York: Viking.

CALIFORNIA DEPARTMENT OF EDUCATION. 2004. California English Language Development Test (CELDT). www.cde.ca.gov/proficiencylevels.

CAPOTE, TRUMAN. 1983. *The Christmas Story*. New York: Knopf Books for Young Readers.

———. 1989. *A Christmas Memory*. New York: Knopf Books for Young Readers.

———. 1996. *The Thanksgiving Visitor*. New York: Knopf Books for Young Readers.

CHAMBERS, AIDAN. 1983. *The Present Takers*. London: Bodley Head.

CHAMOT, ANNA, and MICHAEL O'MALLEY. 1987. *Learning Strategies for Problem Solving*. Reading, MA: Addison-Wesley.

———. 1994. *The CALLA Handbook: How to Implement the Cognitive Academic Language Learning Approach*. Reading, MA: Addison-Wesley.

CHRISTIANSEN, LINDA. 2002. *Reading, Writing, and Rising Up: Teaching About Social Justice and the Power of the Written Word*. Milwaukee, WI: Rethinking Schools.

A Christmas Story. [1983] 2000. Directed by Bob Clark III. Warner Studios. DVD.

CLEARY, BEVERLY. 1983. *Dear Mr. Henshaw*. New York: Morrow.

COHEN, ELIZABETH, and RACHEL LOTAN. 1997. *Working for Equity in Heterogeneous Classrooms: Sociological Theory in Practice*. New York: Teachers College Press.

COLLIER, CHRISTOPHER, and JAMES LINCOLN COLLIER. 1974. *My Brother Sam Is Dead*. New York: Four Winds.

———. 1994. *With Every Drop of Blood*. New York: Delacorte.

COMMISSION ON ADOLESCENT LITERACY. 1999. *Adolescent Literacy: A Position Statement*. Newark, DE: International Reading Association.

COOPER, LOUIS Z. 2002. "Does Your Child Need Professional Help?" *Psychology Today* 35: 76.

CORMIER, ROBERT. [1974] 2004. *The Chocolate War*. New York: Knopf.

CRANE, STEPHEN. 1925. *The Red Badge of Courage*. New York, London: Appleton.

CREWS, DONALD. 1991. *Bigmama's*. New York: Greenwillow.

CUMMINS, JAMES. 1981. "The Role of Primary Language Development in Promoting Educational Success for Language Minority Students." In *Schooling and Language Minority Students: A Theoretical Framework*, 3–49. California State University, Los Angeles: Evaluation, Dissemination and Assessment Center.

CURTIS, CHRISTOPHER PAUL. 1995. *The Watsons Go to Birmingham—1963*. New York: Delacorte.

DAHL, ROALD. 1964. *Charlie and the Chocolate Factory*. Illustrated by Quentin Blake. New York: Knopf.

DANIELS, HARVEY. 1994. *Literature Circles: Voice and Choice in the Student-Centered Classroom*. York, ME: Stenhouse.

DANIELS, HARVEY, and NANCY STEINEKE. 2004. *Minilessons for Literature Circles*. Portsmouth, NH: Heinemann.

DAY, FRANCES ANN. 1999. *Multicultural Voices in Contemporary Literature: A Resource for Teachers*. Portsmouth, NH: Heinemann.

DIAZ, JORGE. 1993. *The Rebellious Alphabet*. New York: Henry Holt.

DICKENS, CHARLES. [1861] 2001. *Great Expectations*. New York: Dover.

DONELSON, KENNTH L., and ALLEEN P. NILSEN. 1996. *Literature for Today's Young Adults*. Boston: Addison-Wesley.

DOUGLASS, FREDERICK. [1845] 1999. *Narrative of the Life of Frederick Douglass: An American Slave*. New York: Oxford University Press.

ELLISON, RALPH. [1947] 1980. *Invisible Man*. New York: Vintage.

ESTES, ELEANOR. 1944. *The Hundred Dresses*. New York: Harcourt, Brace.

Fahrenheit 9/11. 2004. Produced and directed by Michael Moore. 122 minutes. Columbia Tristar. DVD.

FEELINGS, TOM. 1995. *Middle Passage: White Ships/Black Cargo*. New York: Dial.

FILIPOVIC, ZLATA. 1994. *Zlata's Diary: A Child's Life in Sarajevo*. New York: Viking.

FISHER, DOUGLAS, and NANCY FREY. 2004. *Improving Adolescent Literacy: Strategies That Work*. Upper Saddle River, NJ: Pearson.

FLEISCHMAN, PAUL. 1999. *Weslandia*. Cambridge, MA: Candlewick.

FLEMING, CANDACE. 2003. *Boxes for Katje*. New York: Farrar, Straus & Giroux.

FRANK, ANNE. 1958. *Anne Frank: The Diary of a Young Girl*. New York: Globe.

FROST, CHRISTOPHER J. In press. "*Night* in the Interdisciplinary Humanities Course: An Integrative Approach." In *Approaches to Teaching Elie Wiesel's* Night, ed. Alan Rosen. Accessed 27 September 2005, www.units.muohio.edu/aisorg/syllabi/FrostArticle.pdf.

GARCIA, EUGENE. 2001. *Student Cultural Diversity: Understanding and Meeting the Challenge*. New York: Houghton Mifflin.

GARDNER, HOWARD. 1983. *Frames of Mind: The Theory of Multiple Intelligences*. New York: Basic.

———. 1993. *Multiple Intelligences: Theory in Practice*. New York: Basic.

GARZA, CARMEN LOMAS. 1990. *Family Pictures/Cuadros de familia*. San Francisco: Children's Book Press.

GIBBONS, PAULINE. 2002. *Scaffolding Language, Scaffolding Learning: Teaching Second Language Learners in the Mainstream Classroom*. Portsmouth, NH: Heinemann.

GILLIGAN, CAROL. 1982. *Different Voice: Psychological Theory and Women's Moral Development*. Harvard University Press.

GLEITZMAN, MORRIS. 1992. *Blabber Mouth*. Australia: Piper.

GOLDING, WILLIAM. [1954] 1962. *Lord of the Flies*. New York: Coward-McCann.

GOODWIN, DAVID. 1991. *Cesar Chavez: Hope for the People*. New York: Ballantine.

GREEN, BETTE. 1973. *Summer of My German Soldier*. New York: Dial.

GREENFIELD, ELOISE. 1977. *Good News: Formerly "Bubbles."* New York: Coward, McKann & Geoghegan.

———. 1978. *Honey, I Love and Other Love Poems*. New York: Crowell.

———. 1997. *Kia Tanisha Drives Her Car*. New York: HarperFestival.

GREGORY, GAYLE H., and CAROLYN CHAPMAN. 2002. *Differentiated Instructional Strategies: One Size Doesn't Fit All*. Thousand Oaks, CA: Corwin.

HALEY, ALEX. 1976. *Roots*. Garden City, NY: Doubleday.

HAMILTON, VIRGINIA. 1986. *The People Could Fly*. New York: Knopf.

———. 1986. *Zeely*. New York: Aladdin.

———. 1990. *Cousins*. New York: Philomel.

————. 1995. *Her Stories.* New York: Blue Sky Press.

HANSBERRY, LORRAINE. [1959] 1966. *A Raisin in the Sun.* New York: New American Library.

HARRIS, VIOLET. 1997. "Children's Literature Depicting Blacks." In *Using Multiethnic Literature in the K–8 Classroom,* ed. Violet Harris. Norwood, MA: Christopher-Gordon.

HAWTHORNE, NATHANIEL. [1850] 1965. *The Scarlet Letter.* New York: Bantam Classics.

HELLER, JOSEPH. 1961. *Catch-22.* New York: Simon & Schuster.

HENDRIE, C. 2004. "In U.S. Schools, Race Still Counts." *Education Week* 23 (19): 16–19.

HENTOFF, NAT. 1982. *The Day They Came to Arrest the Book.* New York: Dell.

HERNANDEZ, ANITA. 2001. "Expected and Unexpected Literacy Outcomes of Bilingual Children." *Bilingual Research Journal* 25: 301–26.

HERR, MICHAEL. [1977] 1991. *Dispatches.* New York: Vintage.

HERRERA, JUAN FELIPE. 1995. *Calling the Doves.* Emeryville, CA: Children's Book Press.

HERSEY, JOHN. 1946. *Hiroshima.* New York: Modern Library.

HESSE, KAREN. 1997. *Out of the Dust.* New York: Scholastic.

————. 2001. *Witness.* New York: Scholastic.

HIAASEN, CARL. 2002. *Hoot.* New York: Knopf.

HINTZ, CARRIE, and ELAINE OSTRY. 2003. *Utopian and Dystopian Writing for Children and Young Adults.* New York: Routledge.

HO, MINFONG. 1993. *The Clay Marble.* New York: Farrar, Straus & Giroux.

HOOBLER, DOROTHY, and THOMAS HOOBLER. 1995. *The African American Family Album.* New York: Oxford University Press.

HOUSTON, JEANNE WAKATSUKI. 1973. *Farewell to Manzanar.* Boston: Houghton Mifflin.

HOWARD, ELIZABETH FITZGERALD. 1991. *Aunt Flossie's Hats (and Crab Cakes Later).* New York: Clarion.

HUGHES, LANGSTON. 1933. *The Ways of White Folks.* New York: Knopf.

————. 2004. *Vintage Hughes.* New York: Vintage.

HUGHES, MONICA. 1990. *Invitation to the Game.* New York: Simon & Schuster.

HUNT, IRENE. 1964. *Across Five Aprils.* Chicago: Follett.

HURSTON, ZORA NEALE. 1934. *Jonah's Gourd Vine.* New York: Harper and Row.

————. [1935] 1990. *Mules and Men.* New York: Perennial Library.

————. 1938. *Tell My Horse.* New York: Harper

————. 1939 *Moses: Man of the Mountain.* Urbana: University of Illinois Press.

————. 1942. *Dust Tracks on a Road.* New York: Arno Press.

————. 1948. *Seraph on the Suwanee.* New York: Charles Scribner's Sons.

————. 1978. *Their Eyes Were Watching God*. Urbana: University of Illinois Press.

HUXLEY, ALDOUS. 1946. *Brave New World*. London: Harper and Brothers.

HYMES, DELL. 1974. *Foundations in Sociolinguistics: An Ethnographic Approach*. Philadelphia: University of Pennsylvania Press.

INNOCENTI, ROBERTO. 1985. *Rose Blanche*. St. Paul, MN: Creative Education.

JALAVA, ANTTI. 1988. "Mother Tongue and Identity: 'Nobody Could See I Was a Finn.'" In *Minority Education: From Shame to Struggle*, ed. Tove Skutnabb-Kangas and James Cummins, 161–66. Clevedon, England: Multilingual Matters.

JIMENEZ, FRANCISCO. 1997. *The Circuit: Stories from the Life of a Migrant Child*. Albuquerque: New Mexico Press.

KARL, JEAN E. 1981. *But We Are Not of Earth*. New York: Dutton.

KENEALLY, THOMAS. 1982. *Schindler's List*. New York: Simon & Schuster.

KINDLER, ANNEKA. 2002. *Survey of the States' Limited English Proficient Students and Available Educational Programs and Services 2000–2001 Summary Report*. Washington, DC: National Clearinghouse for English Language Acquisition and Language Instruction Educational Programs.

KING, MARTIN LUTHER. [1968] 1999. *I Have a Dream*. New York: Scholastic.

KING-SHAVER, BARBARA, and ALYCE HUNTER. 2003. *Differentiated Instruction in English*. Portsmouth, NH: Heinemann.

KOSS, AMY GOLDMAN. 2000. *The Girls*. New York: Dial Books for Young Readers.

KRASHEN, STEPHEN. 1981. "Bilingual Education and Second Language Acquisition Theory." In *Schooling and Language Minority Students: A Theoretical Framework*, 51–79. Los Angeles: California State University, Los Angeles Evaluation, Dissemination and Assessment Center.

LABOV, WILLIAM. 1970. "The Logic of Nonstandard English." In *Black American English*, edited by P. Stoller (pp. 89–131). New York: Delacorte.

LECLAIR, THOMAS. 1981. "The Language Must Not Sweat: A Conversation with Toni Morrison." *New Republic* 184 (21 March): 25–29.

L'ENGLE, MADELINE. 1962. *A Wrinkle in Time*. New York: Farrar, Straus & Giroux.

————. 1976. *A Wind in the Door*. New York: Laurel Leaf.

————. 1978. *A Swiftly Tilting Planet*. New York: Dell.

LEE, HARPER. 1960. *To Kill a Mockingbird*. Philadelphia: Lippincott.

LESTER, JULIUS. 1998. *From Slave Ship to Freedom Road*. Illus. Rod Brown. New York: Dial.

LEVIN, JOEL, R., and PRESSLEY, MICHAEL. 1981. "Improving Children's Prose Comprehension: Selected Strategies That Seem to Succeed." In *Children's Prose Comprehension: Research and Practice*, edited by C. M. Santa and B. L. Hayes (pp. 44–71). Newark, DE: International Reading Association.

LONG, MICHAEL. 1983. "Native Speaker/Nonnative Speaker Conversation in the Second Language Classroom." *Applied Linguistics* 4: 126–41.

LOVELL, PATTY. 2001. *Stand Tall, Molly Lou Melon*. New York: G. P. Putnam.

LOWRY, LOIS. 1989. *Number the Stars*. Boston: Houghton Mifflin.

———. 1993. *The Giver*. Boston: Houghton Mifflin.

———. 2002. *Gathering Blue*. New York: Laurel Leaf.

———. 2004. *Messenger*. New York: Houghton Mifflin.

LYON, GEORGE, ELLA. 1996. "Where I'm From." In *The United States of Poetry*, edited by Joshua Blum, Bob Homan, and Mark Pellington. New York: Harry N. Adams.

MADONNA. 2003. *The English Roses*. New York: Calloway.

MARZANO, ROBERT J., ET AL. 2001. *Classroom Instruction That Works: Research-Based Strategies for Increasing Student Achievement*. Alexandria, VA: Association for Supervision and Curriculum Development.

MATHIS, SHARON BELL. 1975. *The Hundred Penny Box*. New York: Viking.

McKISSACK, PATRICIA. 1991. *Zora Neale Hurston, Writer and Storyteller*. New York: Enslow.

———. 1992. *The Dark Thirty: Southern Tales of the Supernatural*. New York: Knopf.

———. 1998. *Young, Black, and Determined: A Biography of Lorraine Hansberry*. New York: Holiday House.

McLERRAN, ALICE. 1990. *Roxaboxen*. New York: Lothrop, Lee & Shepard.

MILBURN, MICHAEL. 2001. "Lighting the Flame: Teaching High School Students to Love, Not Loathe, Literature." *English Journal* 90: 90–95.

MILES, BETTY. 1980. *Maudie and Me and the Dirty Book*. New York: Knopf.

MILLER, WILLIAM. 1997. *Richard Wright and the Library Card*. New York: Lee and Low.

MITCHELL, MARGAREE KING. 1993. *Uncle Jed's Barbershop*. New York: Simon & Schuster.

MOCHIZUKI, KEN. 1995. *Baseball Saved Us*. New York: Lee and Low.

———. 1997. *Passage to Freedom: The Sugihara Story*. New York: Lee and Low.

MOJE, ELIZABETH BIRR, ET AL. 2000. "Reinventing Adolescent Literacy for New Times: Perennial and Millennial Issues." In *Re/Mediating Adolescent Literacies*, ed. J. Elkins and A. Luke, 4–14. Newark, DE: International Reading Association.

MORA, PAT. 1997. *Tomas and the Library Lady*. New York: Knopf.

MORE, THOMAS. 1997. *Utopia*. New York: Dover.

MORGAN, DAN. 1992. *Rising in the West*. New York: Knopf.

MORRISON, TONI. 1977. *Song of Solomon*. New York: Knopf.

———. 1987. *Beloved*. New York: Knopf.

———. 1992. *Jazz*. New York: Knopf.

MOYERS, BILL. 1996. "Yearning for Democracy." *In Context* (Fall): 14.

MUNSON, DEREK. 2000. *Enemy Pie*. San Francisco: Chronicle.

MYERS, ANNA. 1997. *The Keeping Room*. New York: Walker.

MYERS, WALTER DEAN. 1988. *Scorpions*. New York: Harper & Row.

NANSEL, TONJA, ET AL. 2001. "Bullying Behaviors Among US Youth." *Journal of American Medical Association* 16: 247.

NATIONAL ASSOCIATION FOR BILINGUAL EDUCATION. 2005. *www.nabe.org*. (February)

NAYLOR, PHYLLIS REYNOLDS. 1991. *King of the Playground*. New York: Maxwell Macmillan International Publishing.

NIETO, SONIA. 1999. *Affirming Diversity: The Sociopolitical Context of Multicultural Education* 3d ed. White Plains, NY: Longman.

O'BRIEN, TIM. 1990. *The Things They Carried*. Boston: Houghton Mifflin.

O'NEILL, ALEXIS. 2002. *The Recess Queen*. New York: HarperTempest.

OATES, JOYCE CAROL. 2002. *Big Mouth and Ugly Girl*. New York: HarperTempest.

OLWEUS, DAN. 1993. *Bullying at School: What We Know and What We Can Do*. Cambridge, MA: Blackwell.

ORWELL, GEORGE. [1945] 1996. *Animal Farm*. New York: Harcourt, Brace.

———. [1949] 1990. *1984*. New York: Signet.

PALINSCAR, ANNE MARIE, and ANN BROWN. 1984. "Reciprocal Teaching of Comprehension-Fostering and Monitoring Activities." *Cognition and Instruction* 1: 117–75.

PALUMBO-LIU, DAVID. 1995. Introduction to *The Ethnic Canon: Histories, Institutions, and Interventions*, ed. David Palumbo-Liu. Minneapolis: University of Minnesota Press.

PARKER, DAVID L. 1998. *Stolen Dreams: Portraits of Working Children*. Minneapolis: Lerner.

POLACCO, PATRICIA. 1994. *Pink and Say*. New York: Philomel.

———. 1996. *Aunt Chip and the Great Triple Creek Dam Affair*. New York: Philomel.

PRESSLEY, M. 2002. "Comprehension Strategies Instruction: A Turn-of-the-Century Status Report." In *Comprehension Instruction: Research-Based Best Practices*, edited by C. Block and M. Pressley, 11–27. New York: Guilford.

RABINOWITZ, PETER J., and MICHAEL W. SMITH. 1998. *Authorizing Readers: Resistance and Respect in the Teaching of Literature*. New York: Teachers College Press.

RAMPERSAD, ARNOLD, ed. 1996. *The Collected Poems of Langston Hughes*. New York: Knopf.

REED, ANGEL. 2003. Personal interview by the authors.

REMARQUE, ERICH MARIA. 1929. *All Quiet on the Western Front*. London: G. P. Putnam.

RICKFORD, JOHN. 1992. "Pidgins and Creoles." In *International Encyclopedia of Linguistics: Volume 3*, ed. William Bright, 224–32. New York: Oxford University Press.

RINALDI, ANN. 1993. *The Fifth of March: A Story of the Boston Massacre*. New York: Gulliver.

————. 1996. *In My Father's House.* New York: Scholastic.

RINGGOLD, FAITH. 1991. *Tar Beach.* New York: Crown.

————. 1992. *Aunt Harriet's Underground Railroad in the Sky.* New York: Crown.

RIVERA, TOMAS. 1995. *Y no se lo Traga la Tierra/ . . . And the Earth Did Not Devour Him.* Houston, TX: Arte Publico.

RODRIGUEZ, LUIS. 1980. *La Vida Loca: Gang Life in L.A.* New York: Touchstone.

ROMAINE, SUZANNE. 1989. *Bilingualism.* Cambridge: Blackwell.

ROWLING, J. K. 1998. *Harry Potter and the Sorcerer's Stone.* New York: A. A. Levine.

SACHAR, LOUIS. 1987. *There's a Boy in the Girls' Bathroom.* New York: Knopf.

————. 1998. *Holes.* New York: Farrar, Straus & Giroux.

SAN SOUCI, ROBERT. 1989. *The Talking Eggs.* New York: Dial Books for Young Readers.

————. 1995. *The Faithful Friend.* New York: Simon & Schuster Books for Young Readers.

SANDERS, SCOTT RUSSELL. 1997. *A Place Called Freedom.* New York: Simon & Schuster.

SANTIAGO, ESMERALDA. 1993. *When I Was Puerto Rican.* New York: Vintage.

SATRAPI, MARJANE. 2003. *Persepolis: The Story of a Childhood.* New York: Pantheon.

SAY, ALLEN. 1999. *Tea with Milk.* Boston: Houghton Mifflin.

SCARCELLA, ROBIN. 2003. *Academic English: A Conceptual Framework.* Santa Barbara, CA: Linguistic Minority Research Institute.

SCHULTEN, KATHERINE. 1999. "Huck Finn: Born to Trouble." *English Journal* 88: 55–60.

SENDAK, MAURICE. 1963. *Where the Wild Things Are.* New York: Harper & Row.

SEUSS, DR. [THEODORE GEISEL]. 1957. *The Cat in the Hat.* New York: Random House Books for Young Readers.

————. 1961. *The Sneetches and Other Stories.* New York: Random House.

SIMON, FRANCESCA. 1999. *Hugo and the Bully Frogs.* London: David & Charles Children's Books.

SIMS BISHOP, RUDINE. 1993. "Multicultural Literature for Children: Making Informed Choices." In *Teaching Multicultural Literature, K–8,* ed. Violet Harris, 39–51. Norwood, MA: Christopher-Gordon.

————. 1997. "Selecting Literature for a Multicultural Curriculum." In *Using Multicultural Literature, K–8,* ed. Violet Harris, 1–19. Norwood, MA: Christopher-Gordon.

SLEETER, CHRISTINE, and CARL GRANT. 1999. *Making Choices for Multicultural Education: Five Approaches to Race, Class, and Gender.* Upper Saddle River, NJ: Merrill.

SMITHERMAN, GENEVA. 1977. *Talkin' and Testifyin': The Language of Black America.* Detroit: Wayne State University Press.

————. 1994. *Black Talk: Words and Phrases from the Hood to the Amen Corner.* New York: Houghton Mifflin.

SOTO, GARY. 1990. *Who Will Know Us? New Poems.* San Francisco: Chronicle.

SPIEGELMAN, ART. 1986. *Maus: A Survivor's Tale: My Father Bleeds History.* New York: Pantheon.

————. 1992. *Maus II: A Survivor's Tale: And Here My Troubles Began.* New York: Pantheon.

SPINELLI, JERRY. 1996. *Crash.* New York: Knopf.

————. 2000. *Stargirl.* New York: Knopf.

————. 2002. *Loser.* New York: Joanna Cotler.

STANLEY, JERRY. 1992. *Children of the Dust Bowl: The True Story of the School at Weedpatch Camp.* New York: Crown.

STEINBECK, JOHN. [1939] 1967. *The Grapes of Wrath.* New York: Viking.

STEPTOE, JOHN. 1987. *Mufaro's Beautiful Daughters.* New York: Lothrop, Lee & Shepard.

STICE, J. E. 1987. "Using Kolb's Learning Cycle to Improve Student Learning." *Engineering Education* 77 (29): 291–96.

STOWE, HARRIET BEECHER. [1851] 1964. *The Annotated Uncle Tom's Cabin.* New York: P. S. Eriksson.

STRASSER, TODD. 2000. *Give a Boy a Gun.* New York: Simon & Schuster Books for Young Readers.

STRICKLAND, KATHLEEN. 2005. *What's After Assessment?* Portsmouth, NH: Heinemann.

SWAIN, MERRILL. 1986. "Three Functions of Output in Second Language Learning." In *Principle and Practice in Applied Linguistics: Studies in Honour of H. G. Widdowson,* ed. G. Cook and B. Seidlehofer. Oxford, UK: Oxford University Press.

TAKAKI, RONALD. 1993. *A Different Mirror: A History of Multicultural America.* Boston: Little, Brown.

TAYLOR, MILDRED D. 1976. *Roll of Thunder, Hear My Cry.* New York: Dial.

————. 1987. *The Friendship.* New York: Dial Books for Young Readers.

————. 1987. *The Gold Cadillac.* New York: Dial Books for Young Readers.

TAYLOR, THEODORE. 1973. *The Maldonado Miracle.* New York: Avon.

TEACHERS OF ENGLISH TO SPEAKERS OF OTHER LANGUAGES (TESOL). January 2004. *ESL Standards for Pre-K–12 Students, Online Edition. www.tesol.org/s_tesol/.*

TERKEL, STUDS. 1997. *Working: People Talk About What They Do All Day and How They Feel About What They Do.* New York: New Press.

THOMAS, JANE RESH. 1994. *Lights on the River.* New York: Hyperion.

TODD, LORETO. 1990. *Pidgins and Creoles.* New York: Routledge.

TOVANI, CRIS. 2000. *I Read It, But I Don't Get It: Comprehension Strategies for Adolescent Readers.* Portland, ME: Stenhouse.

TURIN, ADELA, and NELLA BOSNIA. 1976. *Arturo y Clementina*. Barcelona: Editorial Lumen.

TWAIN, MARK. [1884] 1948. *The Adventures of Huckleberry Finn*. New York: Grosset & Dunlap.

U. S. DEPARTMENT OF EDUCATION. *The Growing Numbers of Limited English Proficient Students: 1991/92–2001/2*. Washington, DC: The National Clearinghouse for English Language Acquisition and Language Instruction Education Programs (NCELA). *www.ed.gov/offices/OELA/*.

VALDÉS, GUADALUPE. 2001. *Learning and Not Learning English: Latino Students in American Schools*. New York: Teachers College Press.

VOLAVKOVA, HANA. 1994. *I Never Saw Another Butterfly: Children's Drawings and Poems from Terezin Concentration Camp 1942–1944*. New York: Schocken.

WALKER, ALICE. 1982. *The Color Purple*. New York: Harcourt, Brace, Jovanovich.

WALQUI, AIDA. 1993. *Sheltered Instruction: Doing It Right*. Unpublished manuscript.

———. 2000. *Access and Engagement: Program Design and Instructional Approaches for Immigrant Students in Secondary School*. McHenry, IL: Delta Systems.

———. 2003. *Quality Teaching for English Learners*. San Francisco: WestEd.

WESTALL, ROBERT. 1987. *Children of the Blitz*. London: Penguin.

———. 1999. *Machine Gunners*. Minneapolis: Sagebrush Bound.

WHITCOMB, MARY E. 1998. *Odd Velvet*. San Francisco: Chronicle.

WHITE, ELLEN EMERSON. 2002. *The Journal of Patrick Seamus Flaherty: United States Marine Corps, Khe Sanh, Vietnam, 1968*. New York: Scholastic.

WIESEL, ELIE. 1960. *Night*. New York: Hill and Wang.

WIGGINS, GRANT, and JAY MCTIGHE. 2000. *Understanding by Design*. Upper Saddle River, NJ: Prentice-Hall.

WILD, MARGARET. 1991. *Let the Celebrations Begin*. New York: Orchard.

WILHELM, JEFFREY. 1997. *You Gotta BE the Book*. New York: Teachers College Press.

WILLIAMS, BRONWYN T. 2004. "A Puzzle to the Rest of Us: Who Is a 'Reader' Anyway?" *Journal of Adolescent and Adult Literacy* 47 (98): 686–89.

WILLIAMS, SHERLEY ANNE. 1992. *Working Cotton*. New York: Harcourt Brace Jovanovich.

WILLIAMS-GARCIA, RITA. 1988. *Blue Tights*. New York: Bantam.

WILSON, AUGUST. 1990. *The Piano Lesson*. New York: Dutton.

———. 1995. *Fences*. New York: Plume.

WILSON, JACQUELINE. 2001. *Bad Girls*. New York: Delacorte.

WOODSON, JACQUELINE. 1990. *Last Summer with Maizon*. New York: Delacorte.

WRIGHT, RICHARD. 1940. *Native Son*. New York: Harper & Row.

———. 1992. *Black Boy (American Hunger)*. New York: Harper & Row.

X, MALCOLM [MALCOLM LITTLE]. 1965. *The Autobiography of Malcolm X*. New York: Grove.

YOLEN, JANE. 2002. *Briar Rose*. New York: Starscape.

ZIMMERMANN, SUSAN, and ELLIN OLIVER KEENE. 1997. *Mosaic of Thought*. Portsmouth, NH: Heinemann.

INDEX